SOLDIER

SOLDIER

RESPECT
IS
EARNED

JAY MORTON

with Boris Starling

HarperCollins*Publishers*

HarperCollins*Publishers*
1 London Bridge Street
London SE1 9GF

www.harpercollins.co.uk

First published by HarperCollins*Publishers* 2020

1 3 5 7 9 10 8 6 4 2

© Jay Morton 2020

Jay Morton asserts the moral right to
be identified as the author of this work

A catalogue record of this book is
available from the British Library

HB ISBN 978-0-00-841815-1
TPB ISBN 978-0-00-841816-8

Printed and bound in Great Britain by
CPI Group (UK) Ltd, Croydon

MIX
Paper from
responsible sources
FSC™ C007454

This book is produced from independently certified FSC™ paper
to ensure responsible forest management.

For more information visit: www.harpercollins.co.uk/green

To everyone who has influenced my life for the better and for the worse. To my family who have always been my family regardless of the shit I put them through. And to you, the reader – I hope my experiences and the lessons I've learned will inspire you to believe there is always more and there is always a way.

CONTENTS

PROLOGUE

MOUNT EVEREST, MAY 2019

I'm in trouble here.

A thin cone of light from my head torch cuts through the darkness. It's just enough for me to see the rocks and snow beneath my feet and in front of my face before the beam peters out and fades, swallowed up by the night. I can only hear three sounds: the wild howl of the wind, the clinking of my carabiners and the ragged gasping of my own breath. I don't know what time it is, other than that it's the middle of the night, the witching hour at which anyone with a modicum of sense would be tucked up in a sleeping bag and tent. It's a long time since I left Camp 1 and a long time till I arrive at Camp 2.

If I ever get there, that is.

Like I said, I'm in trouble. Big trouble. Real trouble. And that's not a figure of speech.

I'm freezing cold, and no matter what I do I just can't get warm. My body's struggling to generate heat, even though I'm wearing all the kit I could find. It's because I haven't eaten or slept enough. I'm so cold I'm not even shivering, and that's not good. Shivering is your body's way of trying to warm itself up. If I could go quicker then perhaps I'd get a bit warmer, but I'm so tired that I need to rest after pretty much every step. It's a vicious circle. I need to move quicker to warm up, but I'm too cold to do anything other than trudge. The slower I go the colder I become, and the colder I become the slower I go. I've got no energy left, absolutely none. Even though my body's trying to work hard – it's a steady climb at an altitude of more than 6,000 metres, where there's half as much oxygen as at sea level – nothing hurts. I can't feel any lactic acid in my legs or muscle burn in my arms. I can't feel anything. That's the problem. It's like someone's turned the tap off or taken the plug out, and there go my last reserves of energy, dribbling away down the drain.

One step. Rest. One step. Rest. One step. Rest. And each time the gap between steps seems to grow just a little. Have to keep going. Want to stop. Want to rest up here a while and get some strength back, though how that's going to happen without warmth or food is

2

anyone's guess. Still. Just stop for a bit, eh? Summon up the old sinews for a final push.

Body shutting down. Mind shutting down.

Through the fog in my brain, I realise that I'm going hypothermic.

There are three stages to hypothermia. First it's mild, where the body is doing all it can to preserve heat: shivering, quick and shallow breathing, elevated pulse rate, contraction of blood vessels. Next comes moderate, where you become confused and forgetful, your speech gets slurred, your reflexes slow down and your fine motor skills start to go. Right now I reckon I'm in the early part of stage two.

And I really don't want to go any further down Hypothermia Highway, because the last stage – and often the terminal one – is severe. It's a gradual shutdown of bodily functions, basically: your heart rate drops, your respiratory rate drops, your blood pressure drops and most of all your core temperature drops. You become so confused that you start to hallucinate, and your senses are so scrambled that quite often you start to take your clothes off because you feel too hot rather than too cold – and taking your clothes off when it's 20 degrees below with a savage wind chill to boot is only going to end one way. Plenty of corpses have been found partially or totally naked on the higher reaches of mountains.

I'm not at that stage yet, but if I stop for too long I will be. Even though I know what might happen, I'm not scared or panicky either. I'm quite chilled, in fact. That's the killer here, that it's so easy to accept, so welcoming and seductive. I could sit down and never stand up. I could lie down and drift off to sleep. All very serene and painless.

A sudden vision comes into my head: all the blokes in Camp 2, just up the mountain from me but right now as remote as the moon, waking up to find that a body's been found just short of their tents. Some poor, stupid bastard who'd tried to get there but had fallen just short.

Some poor, stupid bastard called Jay Morton, in fact. This is my own death I'm seeing.

I made it to Camp 2, of course, or else you wouldn't be reading this (or at least it would have taken the concept of ghostwriting to a whole new level.)

It wasn't the first time I'd faced the prospect of my own death, and I'm sure it won't be the last. That's not me being all macho and full of bravado, but just matter of fact: when you voluntarily put yourself in dangerous situations you accept that sometimes you'll be taken to the edge. As you'll read later in the book, me being alone on Everest that night was actually the least worst option, bizarre as that may sound. I wasn't doing that climb solo and knackered because I wanted to. I was doing it because every possible alternative was more rather than less likely to kill me.

A brief bit of background. I was born in 1984 in the Lancashire city of Preston, and spent my childhood there. Some lads who went on to serve in the Special Forces have real horror stories of being brought up, proper *Oliver Twist* stuff or worse. Mine wasn't anything like that. It was just a pretty normal, unremarkable childhood. I was an adventurous kid who never liked being indoors, and I had a short attention span. These days I'd be diagnosed with ADHD or hyperactivity, but back then I was just a low-level pain in the arse, constantly distracted and getting into trouble. I wasn't a bad kid, and I certainly wasn't a mean kid: I just didn't like school much, and the feeling was pretty mutual. The best times I had at school were on the sports pitch, where I played rugby league (and to any southerners reading who think that league isn't proper rugby, you're very welcome to come up north and say that …).

So I left school as soon as I could, aged 16, and though I went on to college (still in Preston) to study sports science, I jacked that in after a year. Part of it was that I was already earning decent money as a delivery driver, but more importantly I just didn't want to be cooped up within four walls with a lecturer droning on. Delivery driving wasn't the most exciting job in the world, but at least it didn't involve being in an office, which was and remains my idea of hell. It got me out and about, and within reason – I had to do my pick-ups and drop-offs, obviously – I could do my own thing: listen to music, enjoy my own company.

But even then I knew it wasn't a long-term career prospect. I didn't want to be doing that all my life. I wanted to get out and explore, to push and stretch myself. I knew that some of my mates would never leave Preston, would be happy to plough more or less the same furrow from cradle to grave. Good luck to them if that's what they wanted, but I couldn't think of anything worse. That's nothing against Preston in particular: I'd have felt the same way about anywhere. There was a whole world out there: why restrict myself to just one place?

The seeds of what I really wanted to do had been sown years before, when as a young kid I'd gone with my older brother to the library. I wasn't exactly a book-worm, so that visit was a collector's item right there. He showed me a book with a black cover, and on the front was a picture of a bloke with a respirator on and carrying an MP5.

'SAS', it said in big letters.

'What's the SAS?' I asked.

'It's a secret fighting force,' my brother replied. 'They're like spies for Britain.'

I thought that sounded pretty cool.

But of course even as that kid I realised that I couldn't just walk into the SAS. I'd have to join the regular army first to have even a chance (and right from the start I knew it was a small chance, a very, *very* small chance; but I also knew it was the kind of chance which would be entirely in my own hands). I learned that there are two infantry units, the Paras and the Marines, which are kind of a halfway house between the regulars and the SAS. I figured if I could get into one of these then I'd be a little bit further down the road towards my ultimate aim, and for some reason I'd always reckoned that I'd go for the Marines. God knows why: Preston's miles from the sea, and I knew so little about anything maritime that I may as well have been living in the Sahara. But I had my heart set on the Marines, so the Marines it was.

Well, at least until I walked into the recruiting office.

A big sergeant-major looked me up and down, this scrawny kid from Preston. He didn't look impressed. I could hardly blame him. He asked me a few questions. I gave him a few answers. He gave me a booklet.

'Read this, son, and if you're still keen then come back and we can see what you're made of.'

'Thank you, sir.'

I was about to walk out when he asked me one final question.

'Can you do pull-ups?'

'Of course.'

'How many?'

I thought about bullshitting him, but I knew he'd see straight through me. 'One or two, sir.'

'Don't bother coming back till you can do 12.'

12? *12?* I doubted that even Arnold Schwarzenegger could do 12.

I walked out of the Marines office and straight into the army office. I bet they wouldn't ask me to do 12 pull-ups.

They didn't. They tried to get me to join the local regiment, the Queen's Lancashire, but I was having none of it. I wanted to join the Paras, and for me it was that or nothing. No offence to the Queen's Lancashire, which is a cracking outfit, but if it wasn't going to be the Marines then I wanted, *needed* it to be the Paras.

I became a Para in 2004, aged 20. I did four years there, including tours in Iraq and Afghanistan, and then ten years in the SAS (or simply 'The Regiment', as we call it), where I was deployed on multiple Tier One operations (the most elite and secretive ones there are). I've trained in a multitude of different skillsets, including high-altitude parachuting, patrol medic, mountain guide, protective security, mentorship and training … the list gets pretty long.

Since leaving the SAS, I've done lots of different stuff – helped set up companies from scratch, turned my hand to racing cars, climbed some of the biggest mountains in the world, written this book – but the best known of them all is of course appearing on the Channel 4 show *SAS: Who Dares Wins*, in which a bunch of former Special Forces instructors put civilian volunteers through a tough and gruelling selection process. My participation had a bit of a twist, though, as I saw it from both sides, both contestant and instructor. For the first six days I was a contestant, reporting back to the instructors on my fellow contestants: who was going well and who wasn't, who needed taking down a peg or two and who needed a bit of encouragement. Then, in a big reveal, I was brought out as one of the instructors myself, and for the last ten days I worked alongside the other four instructors: Ant Middleton, Jason Fox, Mark Billingham and Ollie Ollerton. The series has been a huge hit ever since it first aired in 2015, and appearing on it has raised my profile in ways I could never have imagined when I was in The Regiment, let alone as that kid looking at the SAS book in the library all those years ago.

My experiences both in the army and outside it have taught me so much about life and how to approach it. Those lessons are what this book is about. I didn't want to write a straight memoir for three main reasons. First, every Tom, Dick and Harry who's ever come within so much as sniffing range of Hereford, the regimental headquarters in Hereford, has written their life story. Second, half of those books belong in 'fiction' rather than 'biography' – for example, the balcony on the Iranian embassy would need to be about the size of Old Trafford to accommodate all those who claim to have been there during the 1980 siege – and I don't want anyone to lump me in with that kind of stuff. Last, but by no means least, I signed the Official Secrets Act, and I take that very seriously. There's a lot of stuff I did which would blow your mind if you knew about it, but legally I can't write about it, and even if I could I wouldn't want to. Those things are secret for lots of sound reasons, and I'm not going to compromise operational security just to make myself look good.

But what I *can* do is take things I learned from those missions and pass them on in ways which don't endanger anyone. Hence the title *Soldier*. When you're a soldier, it's not just a word: it's a way of life, and it's all-encompassing. It's how you live every aspect of that life: the standards you set, the values you uphold, the methods you use and the systems to which you belong. Being a soldier isn't a nine-to-five job. You don't take the role on and off with the uniform, and you don't leave it in the barracks when you go home at night. When I read news reports about 'an off-duty soldier' – well, I know what they mean, but in a very real way as a soldier you're never off-duty. Your duty is your life, and it's with you and in you 24 hours a day.

The army is very keen on acronyms and mnemonics, so I've made one out of that single word 'soldier'. There are seven chapters, one for each letter, and between them they cover much of what soldiering has taught me about various life challenges:

S is for Self: knowing yourself, looking after yourself and pushing yourself.

O is for Opportunity: how to be open to it and maximise it.

L is for Leadership: the importance of it and the best ways to accomplish it.

D is for Danger: the thrill of facing it and the ways to relish rather than fear it.

I is for Intelligence: the twin meanings of the word, intellect and information.

E is for Excellence: how to set, achieve and maintain the highest standards.

R is for Resilience: keeping going through all the setbacks life throws at you.

The lessons I've learned in all seven areas have made me not just a better soldier but also a better person, and the two are intertwined. I hope these lessons help you as much as they've helped me.

SELF

To be one's self, and unafraid whether right or wrong,
is more admirable than the easy cowardice of
surrender to conformity.

Irving Wallace

You can't be your best self until you know yourself. It sounds so obvious put like that, but you'd be surprised how few people really try to know themselves. In many ways, self-knowledge is actively discouraged in our society. It's often seen as self-indulgent navel-gazing, an unhealthy egocentric fixation, rather than something properly worthwhile. 'Finding yourself' sounds very hippy-dippy Californian, and who's got the time or inclination for that kind of stuff – especially in Britain, where we like to think we don't take things too seriously?

Well, we make time for all kinds of stuff which in the scheme of things aren't really that important, so spending a little time on something which is (to use a military term) mission critical is pretty much by definition time well spent. And crucially, this doesn't need to involve a whole lot of angst and agonising, still less a weekly visit to a therapist to unburden yourself of every last childhood trauma. You simply need to apply basic analytical skills, the kind of stuff you do every day in any number of areas almost without thinking.

The best place to start is with a simple personality test. There are several different models around, each with their own strengths and weaknesses and also with their supporters and detractors, but the one I've found most useful is the Myers–Briggs test. This rates you in four main areas:

- How you focus attention or get your energy (extraversion/introversion)
- How you perceive or take in information (sensing/intuition)
- How you prefer to make decisions (thinking/feeling)
- How you orient yourself to the external world (judgement/perception)

You're assigned to one category in each area, which means there are 16 possible personality types. There are no right or wrong answers, no 'better' or 'worse' personalities. I come out as ENFP – extraverted, intuitive, feeling and perceiving personality traits. ('Intuitive' is given the initial 'N' because 'I' is already taken by 'introversion'.) ENFPs are known as campaigners, and among a campaigner's main characteristics (both positive and negative) are the following ten, all of which apply to me:

1. *Charming, independent, energetic and compassionate.* I'll let other people judge me on the first, but the other three definitely apply. Independence and energy were the things which got me in trouble as a kid!
2. *Tends to embrace big ideas and actions that reflect their sense of hope and goodwill towards others.* I'm always keen on new projects, the more ambitious the better, and I like to be around people and look for the best in them. I want to go out and experience things, and if that means stepping out of my comfort zone then so much the better.
3. *Craves creativity and freedom more than stability and security.* This might sound a bit weird coming from someone who spent 14 years in the army, one of the

most stable and secure institutions there is. But remember that almost three-quarters of that time was in the SAS, where ranks matter much less, where free thinking is not just accepted but expected and encouraged, and where pushing boundaries was something which happened pretty much every day. I'd never have lasted that long in the Green Army (what we call the normal, regular army).

4. *Self-esteem is dependent on being able to come up with original solutions. Can quickly lose patience or become depressed if trapped in a boring role.* I left the SAS to do other things – a whole heap of other things – when it became clear that sooner or later I'd be eased into a desk job full of administrative tasks and routine maintenance.

5. *Likes to connect emotionally with others and find what motivates them.* I love being around people and finding out what makes them tick. When you spend months in a windswept, sand-blasted, flyblown FOB (Forward Operating Base) in the middle of nowhere in Afghanistan, with only a handful of blokes for company and the Taliban lobbing mortars on you night after night, you end up becoming pretty tight with your comrades. You have to: your life depends on it. And when you see people in those circumstances, at extremes that most folk will

(perhaps thankfully) never experience, you form bonds which last for ever.

6. *Can't bear to lose that little spark of madness.* This, 100 per cent. Lots of people would tell you my spark isn't that little, but no matter the size, the fact that it's there, and stays there, is what matters.

7. *Would prefer that there be hardly a hierarchy at all.* I touch on this more in the leadership section too, but in essence yes, very much. I love to give and receive good ideas all the time, and I don't care where they come from. Brainstorms among equals are great: I'm genuinely excited to hear different viewpoints and suggestions. The notion that someone should be senior to someone else just because they're older or more experienced is anathema to me. I don't care what title you have: I care who you are and what you bring to the table. I don't respect position, but I do respect the people who've earned that respect.

8. *Intolerant of micromanagement.* Mate, you've told me what you want me to do. Now let me do it. Don't stand over my shoulder or get in my face every five seconds to check up on me: it'll just piss me off and mean I don't do the task properly.

9. *Has difficulty focusing.* This is not just from the restless energy as a child that I mentioned earlier, but also quite a selective thing. If I love something I can

focus on it like a laser, but give me something I'm less keen on but still needs doing and my attention starts to wander. I'm not a great one for admin and all that. I know it has to be done and I do it, but it's a chore rather than something which really satisfies me.

10. *Independent to a fault.* I can be too independent for my own good sometimes. I don't deliberately try to be, but I find myself pushing people away both professionally and personally when I feel that they're encroaching too much on my turf. It's like that Robert De Niro line in the movie *Heat*: 'Don't let yourself get attached to anything you are not willing to walk out on in 30 seconds flat.' I'm not quite that bad (and also, unlike his character in that film, I'm not a bank robber) but, yes, I do see that sometimes it vexes people who don't live their lives like that.

There are two other aspects to my personality which aren't necessarily typical of all campaigners but are definitely me.

The first is how much I need to be outside. It's not just that I don't like being in an office: I don't like being inside. I read an interview once with Gaby Reece, the former volleyball player who's married to the surfer Laird Hamilton. She spoke about how he would come in from the sea and have lunch with her and their children, and though he was fully engaged with them and what they were doing, after an hour or so she would see him start to twitch, because he'd had enough of being inside and needed to be back out on the waves where his soul belonged. The same is true of the ultrarunner Kilian Jornet who lives and trains in Norway: for him it's the mountains rather than the ocean where he finds his grace.

I'm not quite as extreme as either of them, but I definitely get where they're coming from. Nothing would depress me more than working in an office. I just couldn't do it. I used to look at my dad putting on a suit and tie and going to work, and I remember thinking, 'What's all that about?' I've never worn a suit in my life. If I do have to go into an office space even for a few hours I feel the energy being sucked out of me. I'm far more productive on 'working walks', tramping across a heath with my brain in neutral and letting the ideas come to me. Sitting at a screen is, for me, doing stuff that's already been decided and now just needs to be executed. Deciding that stuff needs a different space entirely. This is not to be down on those who like offices. Lots of people do, because they have the personality types which do, and if that's you then knock yourself out. Me? Couldn't do it if you paid me.

The second is a very simple psychological action and reaction: I'm hardwired to do things when someone reckons I can't. The quickest way to get me to do anything is to tell me that it's beyond me. Even if I know that person's not being serious and saying it just to wind me up, I'll still bite. I'm like Pavlov's dog. It comes from the same place as my competitive nature, wanting to be stronger than other people and get one up on them. I don't think there's a single defining moment in my life which made me that way: it's always been there for as long as I can remember, a little bit of insecurity. Back in Preston I was always around the lads who got the girls and I never did. I wasn't unpopular, I don't think, but I wasn't ever super-popular either. So if someone says, 'You can't do this' and I reply, 'Fuck you,' there's a lot behind that 'fuck you'. That's my way of getting not just even but one up. Whatever else other people may or may not be, I'm stronger, I'm faster, I'm tougher, I'm a better soldier.

That little bit of insecurity means I still have impostor syndrome sometimes. I'm doing some racing for the Praga car company in 2021, and when I first went down to Brands Hatch to meet them and try out the cars I felt a bit like, 'What am I doing here?' I've come a long way since I was that kid in Preston, but in some ways I still feel like that kid, and I clearly remember what it was like growing up there. If you'd told the ten-year-old me that in a quarter of a century's time I'd be racing cars round one of the most famous circuits in Britain, I'd have thought you were mental. Yet here I am, and a lot more besides, and that takes some getting used to.

It's not a bad thing to feel impostor syndrome now and then, though, not at all; as long as it's mild, I guess, and as long as I don't dwell on it and let it become debilitating. (You'd be surprised how many people, lots of them much more famous and accomplished than I am, also have it: people who you wouldn't guess in a million years, they seem so confident and sorted.) It keeps me humble and sharp and hungry; makes me keep my eyes and ears open, attuned to learning as much as possible. The moment I think I'm Billy Big Bollocks is the moment I'm sunk.

I like to think of it as being in a big hall full of people doing martial arts. You can tell how experienced and skilful someone is by the colour of their belt. The white belts are the lowest rank, and then the grades go up through yellow, orange, green, blue, brown and black. Which one do I want to be? Most people would say, 'Black belt,' as that's the best.* Not me. I'd rather think of myself as a white belt, with everything to learn and a

* Actually, there are ten separate levels of black belt rather than just the one – the black belt is supposed to signify the start of mastery of the art rather than the end – but let's not go there right now!

lifetime of progress in front of me. Even in an area where I'm experienced, such as soldiering itself, where my actual level of achievement is equivalent to a black belt, my attitude is still that of a white belt. Everyone you meet can teach you something; you just have to be open.

And if this means parking your ego, so be it. Former Navy SEAL commander Jocko Willink says that 'ego is like reactive armour. The harder you push against it, the more it pushes back. You might be afraid that if you subordinate your ego you will get trampled. But that normally doesn't happen because subordinating your ego is actually the ultimate form of self-confidence. That level of confidence earns respect. To put your ego in check, to subordinate your ego, you must have incredible confidence. If you find you cannot put your ego in check because you are afraid it might make you look weak, then guess what? You are weak. Don't be weak.'

This ties in with one of the four tenets of the Special Forces: humility. (The other three are the relentless pursuit of excellence, which I'll discuss in the 'Excellence' chapter; a classless society, which comes under 'Leadership'; and a sense of humour, which is vital in pretty much every walk of life. Army humour in general is pretty dark: Special Forces humour is black, really black. A few years ago a bunch of boffins in Surrey came up with one of the darkest substances known to man and called it Vantablack. That's a pretty accurate marker of Special Forces humour.)

The more you achieve in the Special Forces, the more humble you're encouraged to be. You don't need to tell everyone or lie about your achievements to gain recognition. It's like when blokes talk about sex: nine times out of ten the more they talk about it the less they're having. Special Forces operations are clandestine, not just at the time they're carried out but for many years into the future as well. Only a handful of people in the country even know where you are when you're deployed. You can't tell your friends and family. You certainly can't go round shouting it from the rooftops. So it's not a job for people who like or need to show off. If you want fame, fortune and thousands of people chanting your name, you're in the wrong job.

The flipside of only a handful of people knowing where you are or what you're doing is that every one of those people appreciates the skill and commitment which goes into it. So the satisfaction you have is of a job well done and the quiet approval of those who know what it takes. This encourages you to be humble (and if you're not then you'll soon get it pointed out to you).

With humility comes integrity, and this is something else that, even though others around you will be exhibiting it, must come from within yourself. It's a tough job, what I did. It takes violence to stop violence. You have to take lives without hesitation if need be. As the German philosopher Friedrich Nietzsche said, 'Be careful not to become a monster when tracking monsters.' I joined the army because I believed and believe that it's a force for good in the world: that its values are the right ones and that it protects and reinforces a way of life that's worth fighting for.

But that fight can get pretty down and dirty sometimes. George Orwell said that people 'sleep safely in our beds at night because rough men stand ready in the night to visit violence on those who would do us harm'. In the movie *A Few Good Men*, Jack Nicholson's Colonel Jessup tells Tom Cruise's navy lawyer, 'You want me on that wall, you need me on that wall.' I've been on that wall and I've stood ready in the night, and I've done so with pleasure as it's something I loved doing, but at all times I tried to be a good person while doing it, abiding by the rules of war and keeping not just my professional standards high but my moral ones too.

Clearly as a soldier I went where the politicians sent me. Did Western intervention in Afghanistan and Iraq make those countries better or worse? You can argue the toss till the cows come home. If we did make them better, it was only partially: I don't think anyone would argue that those wars were unqualified successes. But I and pretty much everyone I served with genuinely believed we could bring a better life to those people, and we did everything we could to try to effect that. We tried our hardest, I promise you that.

So, once you know yourself, how do you make yourself better?

Again, the answer is self-focus. Sometimes this can be hard, especially when you're in a competitive situation with other people, as you often are in the army. Take P Company, the final course to become a Para. It's eight tests over five days, it's unbelievably hard, and on it hang the last five months of training. Pass, and that training will have been worthwhile; fail, and it will all have been for shit. I remember standing waiting for the start and looking round at everyone else. They looked so strong and confident, like this would be a walk in the park for them, whereas I felt weedy and was absolutely bricking myself. It wasn't till later that I realised that, of course, they were all bricking themselves and I looked strong and confident. It was a good lesson: never confuse your insides with someone else's outsides. You can't do anything about the latter, but you can do a lot about the former.

I concentrate on my own performance, knowing that if I do that then most (though not all) of the rest takes care of itself. During lockdown, I know that many people found it hard to stay motivated and keep in shape, especially if they relied on going to gyms, which were closed. Physical fitness is a big part of my life, and only illness or injury stops me from getting my workouts in. I couldn't afford to think, 'Oh, it's lockdown, everybody's finding it weird, I'll just sit on the couch and stuff my face with Mars Bars.' It would have bled through to too many other aspects of my life, that sense that it was OK to let things go for a while. Physical inactivity would have massively impacted on my mental well-being, and not in a good way.

So I started every morning the way I always do: with five minutes in a wheelie bin full of water. Yes, you read that right. Five minutes up to my shoulders in cold water. Most people think I'm mad even to consider that: why not just run the shower a bit cold for a few seconds at the end? That's not enough, not for me. Give me a wheelie bin with cold water. I can't start the day without it. If I ever miss it I feel a bit out of whack and off-kilter for the rest of that day. Those five minutes rev me up and set me up the way I need to be. The cold water kick-starts my system, bringing the blood to the surface of my skin and priming me both physically and mentally.*

* If you do want to try this, make sure your wheelie bin isn't in a place where you might get mistakenly taken out and tipped in the back of the garbage truck on bin day.

After that I work out. I had three main routines during lockdown which I could do at home, and which you can do too: all you need is a kettlebell and enough space to run 400 metres around your neighbourhood. The routines all began with warm-up and mobility exercises – stretching, basically – to get the body ready:

Routine 1: 200 press-ups, 200 squats, 200 sit-ups, 200 lunges, 200 burpees.* Feel free to break down the reps into manageable sets. I did this in sets of 50 at a time (50 reps of each exercise × 4), though especially with burpees you may find that sets of 25 are easier.

Routine 2: 20 burpees, 400-metre run; 19 burpees, 400-metre run; 18 burpees, 400-metre run; and so on down to 1 burpee and the last 400-metre run, equalling 210 burpees and 8km running in all. I used a 10kg weighted vest for this.

Routine 3: 100 squats, 90 press-ups, 80 sit-ups, 70 kettlebell deadlifts, 60 burpees, 50 dips, 40 kettlebell lunges, 30 kettlebell cleans, 20 single-arm kettlebell swings,

* A burpee is a squat thrust with an additional stand between each rep. It's one of the toughest and most effective bodyweight exercises there is. It's named after its inventor, the American physiologist Royal H. Burpee. I promise you I'm not making this up.

10 kettlebell snatches and 5 × 100-metre sprints. I used a 28kg kettlebell and a 10kg weighted vest.

You don't need to use the same weight kettlebell or vest (or indeed any vest), or follow these routines slavishly. The important point is that you find what works for you and commit to it. I didn't break off during these workouts to answer the phone, send a few e-mails or check my Instagram feed. I did them properly and with 100 per cent focus. As the saying goes, go hard or go home. (Granted, that loses a bit of its punch when you are already at home, but still ...)

I also run two or three times a week: usually 15k on Mondays and Saturdays and 10k on Wednesdays. I plan these runs around my other workouts, so I often complete a workout in the morning then run in the evening. It's just as important to rest as it is to train, and so I try to train for two days and rest for one, with Sunday always one of those days off and at least one more day in the week too.

I've never felt worse after a workout than before one. Some of the best workouts have been when I'm feeling tired or stale beforehand: some of my best runs have been when the rain's coming down horizontal and the wind is threatening to tear trees up by their roots. I've sat inside lacing up my shoes thinking, 'Nah, not sure I can be arsed today,' and within five minutes I've always been, 'Yeah! Come on!' The buzz I get from doing these kind of sessions is indescribable. You get one body and one life, and I hate to see people let themselves get as out of shape as many seem happy to do nowadays. As Socrates (the Greek philosopher, not the Brazilian footballer) said: 'No man has the right to be an amateur in the matter of physical training. It is a shame for a man to grow old without seeing the beauty and strength of which his body is capable.'

If people think this makes me obsessed – well, 'obsessed' is just a word the lazy use to describe the dedicated. I've always had a relationship with difficulty, always wanted to push myself. I bought myself a weights bench from Argos when I was 16 and my mates were busy copping off with girls in the park (the two things weren't unconnected, obviously). I'd go running even when my mates sacked off and weren't into it. I was never naturally strong or fit, but I enjoyed it.

And keeping on with working out like this means that I don't become content or complacent. 'Content' is a tricky word, because lots of people equate it with happiness. I don't think the two are the same, not at all. I'm a happy person in general, but I'm not content. 'Content' to me implies a settling for something, an unwillingness to keep striving and pushing for new things, greater things. Perhaps it would make my life easier if I were content: settle down, buy a house, have a family, get a steady job. But I'm not made that way. I wonder whether content people are subconsciously scared of failing, because the only way not to risk losing is not to put yourself out there in the first place. Even the most successful people have as many failures as they have triumphs. It's the reason I went on SAS Selection after four years in the Paras, because I wasn't content with what I had. I can't remember who said this, but I remember the quote: 'You can't win world titles when you wake up in silk pyjamas.'

So find what motivates you, whatever it is, and go after that. Say you want to learn how to play the guitar, for example. I'm not particularly motivated myself to learn the guitar, but I will try to implement it into my life by forming a habit. I understand that sooner rather than later there'll be a virtuous circle. The more I play, the better I'll get; the better I get, the more rewarded I'll feel from playing; and the more rewarded I feel from playing the more I'll want to play. Feeling the reward of something motivates me. Getting better at things motivates me. Personal growth motivates me.

So I find motivation through discipline, and having and forming discipline feeds that motivation. It's like with the workouts I mentioned above: I'm motivated to be healthy, and I'm healthy because I've been strict with myself with workout routines and so on. If you're struggling with motivation, then try to imagine the feeling you'll get when you complete the task in question, whether that's clearer headspace, a new level of achievement or an endorphin kick. Imagine that feeling, but also know that there are no shortcuts to it.

Through discipline you can form effective habits, but the first effective habit of all is discipline itself. Discipline is the key to everything when it comes to optimising personal performance. Discipline is the little things you've got to do every day, the little choices you make every day. If you want to be successful, do what you say you're going to do when you say you're going to do it and the way you say you're going to do it. That way you'll persevere. It's every day, not just when you feel like it or for a month or so. The discipline is like being a soldier: you're never off-duty. It's tough to be persistent, and it takes persistence to be tough. Being tough isn't about how many pints you can drink or who you can beat in a fight. It's never giving up, it's always keeping going when you're hanging out of your arse, it's about getting up one more time than you're knocked down. It's about never settling for second best, and never settling for what you are today, because tomorrow you could be better.

Make yourself the best at everything that doesn't require talent. Effort doesn't require talent. Hard work doesn't require talent.

As so often, there are plenty of parallels between sport and the military. Mark McKoy, the Canadian athlete who won the 110m hurdles at the 1992 Olympics in Barcelona, now coaches young sportspeople. 'I tell my young athletes all the time: don't tell me what you're going to do. Show me. I know within a couple of days if you're going to make it or not. I did a session once with two young tennis players. They said they wanted to train with me. I told them that they should meet me at 4 o'clock at the gym and I'd assess them and see what they needed. They showed up at 4.10. I just walked out. They don't want it bad enough.'

Self is also about being true to yourself, no matter what it takes. Sam Warburton, who captained the Welsh and British & Irish Lions rugby teams, had a good example. 'Some of the clubs I played for early in my career used to have initiation ceremonies, and the more outlandish and vile the better: one even involved putting a hole in the bottom of a black bag taken from a public bin and drinking the contents. That wasn't just gross: that was dangerous. As a teenager I'd get so drunk at some of these events that I'd have to be scraped off the floor. I didn't like doing this, but I was young and the other players were older and more experienced, so I went along with it for a while.

'Then one day I just thought, *I'm not doing this anymore. I'm not drinking at these things*. I got the piss ripped and called a shit bloke, but I stood my ground: and when I did, there were always other people who'd join me and say, 'I'm not drinking either.' They'd seen me stand up for myself, and that made them want to do the same for themselves. And in the end most people respect you for that, no matter how much grief they might give you at the time.'

This nod towards other people leads me on to one of the biggest things for me: drains and radiators. Basically, people can be divided into two categories: drains, who sap your energy and try to make you see things in a negative light; or radiators, who provide you with warmth and positivity. The divide is not always clear-cut – not everyone is an extreme at either end, of course, and sometimes circumstances can make people feel and act differently from their 'normal': even the most positive people can have down days – but it's there more often than not. It's at heart a 'glass half-full/glass half-empty' dichotomy, but it's much more than that too. Radiators have an infectious energy which makes people feel good about themselves. Drains suck the life out of you, slowly but surely. You end a conversation with a radiator feeling better than you did to start with; it's the opposite way round with a drain. Radiators look for silver linings in every cloud: drains look for the cloud itself.

How can you tell which is which? Well, most of the time it's pretty obvious, and can start even before you're in their presence: do you look forward to seeing someone or not? But if it's not obvious, then see what happens when you suggest a course of action to someone. I had this all the time in the military: there was always an exercise to do, an operation to plan, a training block to complete. The course of action doesn't have to be even anything tricky or risky, just something as simple as a weekend away or a new way of doing things at work. What's their instant reaction? Do they say, 'Yes, that sounds great' or is their default to look for the holes and the problems? Radiators radiate positivity, drains display negativity. It's not a question of whether or not what you've suggested is in itself a good idea, but the way in which people instinctively respond to it. Some people want to find ways of making things happen, others want to find ways of not making things happen.

Typical drain behaviour includes:

- putting you on the defensive by criticising you. It doesn't matter what the criticism is – something you've done, something you haven't done, who you are – just that it's there right from the start;
- pointing out all the things you've done wrong;
- topping your problems with worse ones (usually their own) and your achievements with better ones (usually someone else's) – if you say you've been to Tenerife, they know someone who's been to Elevenerife;
- gossiping which involves snide remarks, schadenfreude and portraying the people being discussed in a bad light;
- making excuses for why they can't do something – I've got the wrong trainers on, I'm tired, didn't get much sleep last night, did too much in the gym bullshit.

Typical radiator behaviour is, logically enough, pretty much the opposite:

- looking for areas in which to praise and encourage you;
- pointing out things you've done right and successes you've had;

- listening to your problems with compassion and constructive advice;
- sharing good news about other people, and respecting things that really matter (emotions, health) more than the things which don't (material things, wealth).

Something that bothers me is this: do drains know they're drains? Surely if you did know you were a drain you'd do anything in your power not to be one (unless you have a personality disorder, I guess). After all, it's not as if drains actually gain the energy they leach from their victims, because if they did they'd turn into radiators sooner or later. Or do drains see themselves as realists, providing much-needed reality checks to radiators and their unrealistic flights of fancy? If so, you can be a realist – and indeed you need to be – without being a drain. A drain will be negative about everything and sometimes be right, in that a given project won't pass muster. A radiator will say, 'I really like what you're trying to do here, but I think this particular approach is wrong for x, y and z reasons: but let's see if there's any way we can fix those.' There has to be some balance here. If all you ever want is love and affection, get a dog.

Of course, you want as many radiators around you and as few drains. This is not just an academic exercise: it's vital to your energy levels, your self-esteem and your ability to maintain your best sense of self. Constant exposure to drains can make you doubt yourself and lose confidence in both your abilities and your judgement. Even the strongest-minded and most independent person takes cues from those around him or her, and you'd have to be either unbelievably tough or a hermit to remain totally immune to constant drain exposure.

But sometimes it's impossible to avoid drains: they might be family members or colleagues. Even in the Special Forces, and certainly in the Green Army, they exist. If so, there are several things you can do to minimise the effect they have on you. First, and most simply, just reduce the amount of time and contact as much as you can. Second, refuse to engage when they start to become negative. Don't get sucked down into arguing about negative things or give them the chance to take the conversation into spirals of bad energy. It takes two to play any game, and if you flatly refuse to get drawn in then that leaves them many fewer avenues for complaining and criticising. Third, maintain a sense of humour: allow yourself a quiet smirk when you see their well-worn tactics being wheeled out for the hundredth time. All these will help you plug the drain and make sure you don't get infected too.

I've served with and under both sorts of man, and the difference is night and day. I'll expand on this more in the leadership chapter, but in an environment as tight-knit and high-pressured as an army unit – especially a Special Forces unit – you simply can't afford to have drains, and when they are around what tends to happen is that people shy away from them and exclude them as far as possible, which may solve the immediate problem but ends up causing many more.

On Selection there was this one guy who was a massive gobshite. He thought he knew it all, and every day he'd tell us what was coming and how to deal with it, because his dad had been in the SAS. (As it turned out, that was a crock of shit: his dad had done Selection but failed, just as this guy would, so it obviously ran in the family.) Perhaps he thought he was being a radiator and helping us, but actually whenever he opened his mouth people just switched off as none of us had the time, energy or inclination to listen to his bullshit. It's rather like sheep and sheepdogs. Sheep will gravitate to a sheepdog, but sometimes the other sheepdogs realise quicker than the sheep that the dog in question is all bark and no bite. That's what it was like with this guy, at least to start with: there were a few of the younger, greener guys who hung on his every word, but one by one they all saw the light and drifted away. You see it too on the former Special Forces circuit. Like I said in the Prologue, the secretive and elite nature of what we do makes this prime bullshit territory for the unscrupulous. It's easy to hold yourself up as a hero to the man in the street, who has no reason to know any better, but those in the know really are aware who's on the level and who isn't.

All these – knowing yourself, making the most of yourself, gravitating towards radiators rather than drains – will help you become a better you. Finding what you love doing is the greatest form of wealth there is.

OPPORTUNITY

Don't wait for the right opportunity. Create it.

George Bernard Shaw

Everything I've done has been because I've taken opportunities when they've arisen. But it's more than just grabbing at things when they come along. It's a three-stage process: encounter, recognise and exploit. Encounter those opportunities, recognise them as such and exploit them as best you can.

First, *encounter*. You have to put yourself in the right place, both internally and externally. Internally means that you have to clarify your goals and know what you're looking for. Before I was in the army, I wanted to be in the Paras. When I was in the Paras, I wanted to be in the SAS. When I left the SAS, I wanted to do things which would stretch and challenge me. Any opportunity which came along would have had to have fitted into these parameters. Being offered the chance to go on an accountancy course wouldn't have been a good opportunity, not for me: it would have played to my weaknesses rather than my strengths.

Externally means being close by opportunities when they come; not necessarily close by physically or geographically, but in terms of having access. And that access more often than not means people. The more people you deal with, the more people you have in your network, the greater your reach and the greater your possibilities. Say I decided to cycle across America and wanted someone to manage that project: drive a support vehicle, deal with the media, get sponsorship and so on. I could advertise online, but that would get me thousands of applications which I wouldn't have the time to sift through. Or I could ask around people who've done that kind of thing, and they might recommend someone to me – which would in turn make me more likely to hire that person, if they came with a personal recommendation. The more people who know you, the more likely you are to be recommended for stuff.

Second, *recognise*. Opportunities don't always come neatly packaged and nicely wrapped with a neon sign saying 'OPPORTUNITY' in large letters, and so they're not always obvious at the time. Indeed, the one which arguably changed my life more than any other was something which I initially didn't want to do and was disappointed to have it presented to me as the only option. Little did I know! It's easy to look at a situation and see what it is at present: it's much harder to look at a situation and see what it could be in the future. It's like renovating a house. Some people just see the rooms as they are; others can envisage the transformation. The gap between current reality and future potential is often where the opportunities really lie. I try to look below the surface and beyond the horizon to see if something which may seem unpromising at first glance actually has hidden treasures. This curiosity unearths opportunities where other people might not see them.

But you also have to find the right balance. If you're determined to see opportunities at every turn then that can be counterproductive: not only might you mistake something which isn't really worthwhile for a genuine opportunity, but you might also miss all the good things in your life as it stands as you'll be too busy thinking the grass is greener. Think of it like setting out on a beautiful walk across the moors in early evening and taking a camera with you. If all you can think about is trying to take a brilliant photo, you'll miss all the things which make the walk worthwhile in the first place: stretching your legs, being outside with nature, seeing animals. What you need to do is keep your mind open without trying to force things. If you get the chance to take that brilliant photo then that's great. If not, then it wasn't supposed to be and you've still enjoyed the walk. Opportunities don't come every day, but they do come.

Third, *exploit*. Whether or not you take advantage of them is a matter of attitude, which is at least partly determined by whether you're a drain or a radiator. A drain will see the negative in everything, and will therefore miss opportunities sooner or later. A radiator, far more open to new ideas, is correspondingly far more likely to recognise an opportunity as such and to grasp it. Your attitude when opportunity presents itself is a large factor in whether that opportunity will make your life better or not. 'What if I fall?' you might ask yourself; to which my reply would be, 'But what if you soar?' To achieve anything in life you need to take a chance: you don't stand a chance if you won't take a chance. I fear boredom and mediocrity more than I fear failure.

I'm lucky that my personality encourages me to exploit new opportunities. I'm more chaos than order: I like spontaneity and flexibility. If you like order and something happens to threaten that order, you find it harder to adjust; but if you embrace chaos and accept that it's part of life then it's much easier to transform. So I've always been up for new experiences, and I've always tried to go into them with my eyes wide open and take what I can get from them. Sometimes they've been genuinely transformative, sometimes they've been fun but fundamentally lightweight, and sometimes they've been disappointing. But in none of those cases did I know what would happen until I tried it. If it's a disappointment, well, that's only a few hours out of your life. By the same token you've probably 'wasted' the same amount of time already this week watching a TV programme you didn't really enjoy, been stuck in traffic or waiting for a delivery which has turned up late. It's always better to regret something you have done than something you haven't; it's always better to know than to wonder. The only true failure in life is not trying.

There's risk in everything, and it's easy to let that risk seem paralysing and send you scurrying for the safety of the status quo. Sometimes that's the sensible choice: if the dangers of a given course are too great, or if there's simply not enough upside to make the effort worthwhile. But a simple, dispassionate weighing up of the pros and cons of any opportunity will give you a sense of whether it's worth proceeding with. Calculated risks shift the odds in your favour.

I can think of so many opportunities which have come my way, but three of them have been bigger and more influential than all the rest put together.

Number one was my first deployment in Afghanistan with 3 Para in 2006. I'd been a Para for two years by then, and I thought I was a soldier. Only when I got to Afghanistan did I realise I wasn't, not yet, not really. Oh, I had the maroon beret and the wings, I'd passed all the tests, and in technical terms I was a soldier, but it's only when you actually experience combat that you realise what soldiering's all about. There are so many facets to being a soldier, and only combat properly tests them and brings them out. I'd been to Iraq for three months the year before but that had been really quiet with not much action at all. This was totally different. We flew into Bastion and from there took CH-47 choppers to Now Zad. The moment my feet touched the ground I heard the crack of the first round over my head. Welcome to Now Zad. Machine-gun fire, small-arms fire, you name it, it was going off. We just looked at each other and laughed: this was it, this was what we'd trained so long and so hard for, and now we could see what we were made of. We ran for cover, located where the rounds were coming from and started firing back. All the training just kicked in. The firefight lasted pretty much the whole day, and it was brilliant. Seriously. I was in a proper scrap, I was sweating, I was part of a team, down on my belt buckle as I took and returned fire. I was young and full of testosterone, and now I could prove myself the way I'd always wanted to. I was, at long last, a soldier.

And that's how it was for the whole of the six months, pretty much just bullet for bullet, endless high kinetic energy firefights. It was before the Taliban really got into all the improvised explosive devices (IEDs), which really changed the nature of the fight, making it much more cautious but also much more vicious. This was more or less straight firefights one after the other, literally going out day after day and getting into scraps. Every contact we had with the enemy was in a weird way so pure, because it was such a binary environment. There were just two types of people there, the ones trying to kill you and the ones trying to keep you alive. There was none of the clutter of ordinary life: no social media, no messages from girlfriends or your mum, no final payment bills mounting up, no pissed twats wanting to have a go at you in a nightclub at two in the morning. Just you and your mates.

I felt that this was where I'd been meant to be all along. I wasn't scared, quite the opposite. I remembered something I'd heard Ayrton Senna once say – that people thought it was all calm before a race started and then all sound and fury when the green light went and two dozen cars hammered towards the first corner, but in fact for him it was quite the opposite. The race was where he felt calmest and most connected, because that was his place. Everything else just faded away. That's how I felt in contact: that everything else had just faded away.

I look back on that 2006 tour and see it as one of the best ones I ever did, either with 3 Para or The Regiment. It changed me as a person and made me grow up a hell of a lot. I must have done ten years' worth of growing up in six months. It was such an intense environment that everything seemed on fast forward, with so many life-changing experiences crammed into such a short space of time. They weren't all positive ones, of course. Sometimes you learn more from the setbacks than you do from the good times. One of the men I most looked up to in the world, Bryan Budd, was killed on that tour (I'll talk about him more in 'Danger'.) Another guy I was out there with shot three Taliban in one contact, and even half an hour later he looked different. The very act of taking those lives had changed him physically. I bumped into him a few years ago and he still had that look in his eyes. When Ross Kemp did his documentary on the Royal Anglians a few years ago, a few of those lads had the same look: the thousand-yard stare, as they called it in Vietnam. I asked my mate if he wanted to come for a drink. 'Mate, I don't drink anymore,' he replied. 'I can't.' His life changed just as much as mine did, but in very different ways. He wasn't lucky. His opportunity turned sour. There's always the chance of that, and you have to accept it.

The second great opportunity came when I joined the SAS. This must sound obvious, given the elite nature of The Regiment and the fact that so few people get to experience life there, but I chose those words – 'when I joined the SAS' – deliberately. The opportunity wasn't joining The Regiment itself: it was the troop I was allocated to.

The Regiment is divided up and I ended up specialising in mountain. I'd never climbed and never been into any of that stuff so it wasn't my first choice, not at all. The Brecon Beacons during selection were probably the highest mountains I'd ever been on. I'd certainly never done any hardcore stuff in the Alps or the Himalayas. Despite that, it turned out that specialising in the mountains was the best thing that ever happened to me. After I'd been in The Regiment for a few years, I went to Germany and trained to a high level to operate in the mountains. My training was divided into two parts – summer and winter – and you cover everything you'll ever need: the theory and practice of climbing, medical training, meteorology, leadership technology, orientation in the mountains, material and safety knowledge, skiing, mountain rescue, avalanche studies, snow studies and even avalanche blasting. It was magic, and I put it down as one of the best things I've ever done. I loved pretty much every day of it: there was always something new to learn, always a fresh challenge, and of course most of it took place in some of the most beautiful scenery anywhere in the world.

One day I climbed up to a high ridgeline with a mate who was doing the course with me. It was a long climb, four or five hours, and when we got to the top it was indescribably serene: clear blue sky, peaks sticking up out of the snow like teeth and stretching away to the horizon in every direction. We sat there with some food and coffee, and it was like a switch had been flicked.

I suddenly saw things not just differently but more clearly. Before I'd done the mountain course I'd been very career-driven, but strictly within army terms. I'd known where I wanted to go and what I wanted to be: team leader of a troop, sergeant-major of a squadron, that kind of thing. But now my outlook was changing. I was thinking that there was more to this world than just being in the army all my life. In some ways it was the same thought I'd had back in Preston all those years ago while driving my delivery van around, but it was also different: because even though I'd seen lots of the world and done things very few people get to do, I was still restless, and even the most exciting job is just a cage if you stay in it long enough and shy away from change. The mountain course was exposing me to something else: something a little more spiritual, perhaps. I knew that there was more stuff out there that I wanted to explore, and Afghanistan was dying off, and something began eating away in my head.

I was asked to climb K2, an expedition sponsored and approved by The Regiment. I was partnered with a geezer called John, who'd been in The Regiment himself but had been invalided out when a helicopter had landed on the wagon he'd been in and flipped it. His knee had gone the wrong way forward, meaning his toes were touching the front of his hip. He'd spent two and a half years in rehab, and had gone on to set up several successful companies and make a lot of money. Now he wanted to climb K2 with me and raise some money for a charity that he was close to. K2 isn't as high as Everest but it's a lot harder to climb – most climbers would say that it's the toughest of all the great Himalayan peaks, perhaps along with Annapurna – and it would be a great test of everything I'd learned in Germany.

By way of training for K2 we attempted to summit Manaslu, the eighth-highest mountain in the world at 8,163 metres, whose name means 'mountain of the soul'. We didn't make it for a number of reasons, which

I expand on in 'Excellence', and after that we decided to shit-can the K2 plan and shoot for Everest itself in 2017.*

There's a lot of talk about how Everest has been cheapened by the sheer numbers of people who climb it these days; a photo (taken by a close friend, Nims 'Dai' Purja) showing hundreds of people waiting to summit, lined up as though in a supermarket queue, went viral last year and caused quite some controversy. There's some truth in this argument. Mountains are dangerous places at the best of times, and you don't want people up there who don't know what they're doing, as that makes them dangerous too. In purely technical terms there are harder mountains out there, but for any serious climber Everest is still a massive goal. It's so famous, there's so much history, and most of all there's the simple fact of it being the highest peak in the world. And the idea that it's in any way 'easy' just isn't true. It's not easy and it never will be: simply being that high demands vast levels of effort and concentration, not to mention luck. As the old Nepalese saying goes, you never conquer Everest – you just get up there while her back's turned.

* This wasn't the ascent which involved my night-time climb between Camps 1 and 2 in the Prologue. That took place two years later.

John and I prepared properly. We did refresher training, John built a climbing wall in his garage and we acclimatised slowly, taking a few extra days to make it up to Base Camp. People are often in a mad rush to make it up to Base Camp, and then when they get there they just have to sit around in shit conditions waiting for the weather to clear, so we figured we may as well take our time. Basically, we did everything to tilt the odds in our favour as much as we could, and if after all that it still didn't happen then that would just be one of those things and we could live with it.

From Camp 1 to Camp 2 should have been a relatively easy day: the ascent is reasonably gentle, the path is pretty straight, and you can see Camp 2 pretty much all the way out, which is a psychological boost. But actually it was a really hard day. The problem was that the landscape is basically a big U-shaped bowl called the Western Cwm which catches the sun and reflects it from all angles, and that really cut us. The air temperature itself wasn't too bad, but with the sun beating down it felt so hot. We were exhausted and dehydrated, and it seemed to take for ever – though not half as long as it would two years later in pitch black, when I'd be begging for even the tiniest scintilla of light or warmth – and we decided to stay an extra night at Camp 2 to recover.

From there it was pretty plain sailing to Camp 3 and then to Camp 4, the latter at almost 8,000 metres and therefore within the so-called Death Zone, where there's not enough oxygen to sustain you for more than a short period. We had oxygen canisters, of course, but there's a limit to how many you can carry. We got to Camp 4 at about teatime and thought we'd rest for a few hours before starting out for the summit at around 8pm, but the wind had got up so much that we knew there was no way we could summit unless it abated. The tent we were due to stay in had been totalled by the gale, so we put another one up, boiled some water and necked some electrolytes. It's hard to eat or sleep properly at this altitude as the human body begins to break down, but you have to try to get that nutrition and rest as best you can. Now and then I'd put my hand out of the tent to see if the wind was still howling, which of course it was – I could hear the damn thing, after all – but I figured if I kept checking then maybe by force of will I could get it to calm down.

I dozed off for a couple of hours. When I woke it was about 7pm, and pitch black. I put my hand out again, and though the wind was still up it felt less savage than it had been, and certainly the air seemed to be quite a lot warmer than before. We decided to go, and if the wind was too bad we'd turn round and come back.

Lacing my crampons on with numb fingers, I reminded myself to control the controllables and try not to worry about the rest. If the wind pushed us back then so be it; if it let us through then also so be it.

We climbed all night. I was quicker than John, so I went on ahead. At The Balcony, just shy of 8,500 metres, I sat down and watched the sun come up, tentatively poking its head above the horizon and spraying the mountains in swathes of pink and orange as it climbed into the sky. It was, I think, the most beautiful thing I'd ever seen. The wind had dropped to nothing, there wasn't a cloud in the sky, and I could see the curvature of the earth as it fell away around and beneath me.

I could have sat there all day, but these were the most perfect conditions for summiting and I couldn't waste them. I kept on climbing, across the Cornice Traverse and then up and over the Hillary Step, which has fixed ropes and can only accommodate one climber at a time. The climbing up until then had been super-easy – I'd climbed harder routes in the Alps, I really had – but the Step is tricky and I knew I couldn't afford to underestimate it. Those fixed ropes were all well and good, but one of the first rules of mountaineering is that you don't use a rope as your primary safety unless you can personally vouch for its integrity. I didn't know who'd fixed that rope, how many times it had frozen and thawed, how long it had been up there, how close to failure it was, or anything else. Sure, the odds on it failing at the precise moment I was on it were pretty slim, but if the worst happened then it was a mile's fall either side. Easy if you have a parachute. Not so much fun if you don't. And I was on my own with no Sherpa or anyone else around due to the high winds at Camp 4.

The last few feet to the summit were marked by prayer flags, discarded oxygen canisters, mementoes left by climbers and some scientific equipment; and then I was there, on top of the world. A couple of Korean climbers were already there. I unfurled my A Squadron flag, they took a picture of me – blurry, as it turned out; thanks a bunch, lads – and then they started their descent and I was left on my own.

I unclipped myself and just took it all in. I'd done it. I'd fucking done it. There are seven billion people on the planet, and I was higher than every last one of them. The sense of achievement was almost indescribable. It was a profound satisfaction, a glow deep in my soul of having committed to something hard and done it, but it was more than that too, and to this day I still don't think I have the words to do it proper justice. Nick Faldo was once asked how it felt to win the Open, and he said it was a question he couldn't answer. If you hadn't done it then you could never know what it felt like, not truly; and if you had done it then you didn't need to ask.

The view from the summit is a 360-degree one, so I oriented myself until I was facing in the direction of Preston. I'd come a long way from there, in every way, but it had also been a journey of a hundred separate steps: I hadn't just left Preston and gone straight to the top of the world. As in any walk of life, if you look towards the summit before you're ready then you'll get discouraged and be tempted to give up. One step at a time is the only way to get there; and when you do get there, that photo you put on Instagram or wherever shows only a snapshot of the end product, not all the time and effort and resilience which went into it. As John F. Kennedy said about the aim of the Apollo programme to land a man on the Moon, we choose to do these things not because they are easy but because they are hard.

That summit, a direct result of the second great opportunity I'd taken, also led inexorably on to the third great opportunity, even if again it didn't happen immediately. I'd climb Everest again two years later, and though it wasn't as good an experience as the first time – just like my second tour in Afghanistan with 3 Para hadn't been as good as the first – it solidified for me what I wanted to do and, just as importantly, what

I didn't want to do. I came back from that first summiting to train some of the counter-terrorism boys, and I realised that sooner or later if I stayed in The Regiment I'd be sat up in ops behind a desk, wearing uniform, clean-shaven, sending shit e-mails about people leaving doors open. I didn't want to train or teach people, and I didn't want to write reports all day long. None of that energised me, and if that was the career path in The Regiment – and it was – then I didn't want a part of it. I didn't want to end up a dinosaur, one of those guys whose whole identity is wrapped up in The Regiment and who can't exist without it. Oh, it would have been so easy to stay, don't get me wrong – unless you fuck up on a royal scale you're never going to get fired – but easy and opportunity don't make natural bedfellows.

So I walked into my commanding officer's office and signed off. It was one of the hardest things I'd ever done. This place had been my life for the past decade, but I could feel in my bones that it was time to move on. I'm not one of those guys who always wants to hang around somewhere or keep going back there once that time in my life has passed. When I'd gained Selection for The Regiment, I went back to the 3 Para barracks in Catterick just once, to get the stuff I'd left there. That's the last time I set foot in the place. It had been a great time, but it had come and gone, and now I felt the same about The Regiment. Been there, done that, bug out.

I had some stuff lined up, including an 'in' on the ThruDark clothing company with my mates Staz and Louis who'd been with the SBS (again, more on that in the 'Excellence' chapter), but going from Hereford to Civvy Street it was still a tricky period, and it took me some time to adjust. In one fell swoop I'd gone from being an integral part of a squadron and a critical key component in a troop, surrounded by like-minded forward-thinking individuals who relied on me the same way I relied on them, to sitting in a flat in London with an exorbitant rent blowing holes in my savings and nothing concrete to fall back on. It was a little scary, but that's the point of stepping out of your comfort zone.

And being free and available led me to my big break – my third opportunity – which was of course getting asked to be on *SAS: Who Dares Wins*. The series had been running for a few years, and the first I'd heard of it had been back in the early days when I'd been in the sauna in Hereford and a couple of the lads had been talking about it. They were quite down on it, perhaps not surprisingly. There's always a big contingent in Hereford who think that The Regiment should remain as secretive as possible and that any books, TV shows or the like about it, especially involving former members, are beyond the pale.

I wasn't so sure. For a start, half of the lads acting as instructors had been in the SBS rather than the SAS, despite the show's title. (The SAS always get top billing no matter what in these situations: it's much more famous than the SBS, which pisses the SBS boys off no end.) Second, it wasn't as though they were giving away secrets, so they weren't doing us a disservice. If anything, they were helping us. The show was hugely popular, and as a recruiting tool it seemed a pretty good one, even if that wasn't the show's intention. It wasn't just that some likely young lads watching would think this looked cool – rather like I had with that library book – and in a few years' time would end up being Tier One operators. It was also that it could help in a less tangible way too. The defence budget is always being cut, and the Ministry of Defence has to fight for funding just like every other government department does. Anything which can help show the value of our Special Forces, and by extension our armed forces, has to be a good thing. There are plenty of programmes about policemen, teachers, doctors and lawyers, after all, and I bet the Home Office and the Departments of Education, Health and Justice don't complain about those.

Besides, I figured that at heart the show isn't really about the SAS at all. It's about putting civilians under similar stressful scenarios that Special Forces guys go through, and bringing the narrative through in that. The show looks to inspire people to get out in every way: out of their homes into the great wide open, out of their routines, out of their comfort zones. So many of the recruits, even those who didn't make it to the end, said it changed and inspired their lives. It seemed a positive show which taught positive qualities – discipline, fitness, health – and as an antidote to something like *Love Island*, which to me is not just vapid and vacuous but actively promotes negative qualities, such as judging people purely on their looks and setting them against each other in the name of drama, it seemed a pretty good thing all round.

It was ThruDark which gave me the opening to *Who Dares Wins*, which goes back to my point earlier in the chapter about putting yourself out there as much as possible. We'd been asked to supply some clothing to the programme, and when we met the producers they said they were looking for another instructor and asked if I was interested in applying. Sure, I said. I'd met Foxy a few times and had chats with him about the show, so I kind of knew how it was good for him. I did a few interviews with the production team and then went on a surfing holiday to Portugal. While I was there, the producers rang and said that they wanted me to do it but just needed to check with Hereford that it wouldn't break the Official Secrets Act.*

My stomach leapt and sank all at the same time. On the one hand, I really wanted to do the programme and was thrilled that they'd asked me. On the other, I knew that lots of people in Hereford would see this as some kind of treachery. I didn't see it that way at all, but I knew they would. This is one of the unavoidable things about taking opportunities – they often come in forms which piss other people off, whether or not they are directly at those people's expense. To an extent this is unavoidable, and you have to be prepared to cop the shit if you think it's worth it, but that doesn't mean you have to like it.

Ah fuck, I thought. Not to be big-headed, but I knew I had a good reputation down in Hereford. I had solid relationships with people, I'd always got decent reports, and in general I was held in pretty high regard. I'd worked ten years for that reputation and those relation-ships. With some people I knew that wouldn't change, but with others it definitely would.

---

* It wouldn't have, obviously, or else none of the other instructors would have been allowed to do it either, but the producers were still legally and morally obliged to check.

Next time I came in from a few hours on my surf-board, my phone was lit up like a Christmas tree. 'Jay, what the fuck are you doing?' was the general gist of the text messages. 'This isn't what someone in the SAS does, especially not one as credible as you.' I found out later that quite a few of my mates had been questioned to see whether they knew about this before it was announced, but I'd deliberately kept it secret. It was this that pissed people off, I realised: a combination of being kept in the dark and the blowback they were getting from higher ranks who thought they must have known and didn't believe them when they said they didn't. And so, even given the way that text messages can flatten someone's tone by removing the nuance of voice and body language, the vibes coming through to me were pretty hostile. It wasn't, 'Can we chat, we just want to talk things through and check you're making the right decision?' It was, 'You're a cunt.'

I reminded myself of the old adage that the people who mind don't matter and the people who matter don't mind. I was clear in my own head that I was doing nothing wrong. If someone wanted to disagree with my choice but still be my mate because sensible adults don't have to see eye to eye on everything, then that was fine. But if someone was going to write me off totally just because of that, then as far as I was concerned they could get fucked. The more messages I got, the less I cared. And then suddenly, and a little bizarrely, a whole lot of supportive ones came in, as though all those who disapproved had blown themselves out and left the field clear for those who were happy for me. Either way, what was done was done.

The producers didn't want me to join the DS (directing staff – the instructors) right away. No: they wanted me to be a contestant, but one with a difference. I would be a mole, reporting back to the DS on the contestants. The DS wanted someone in at ground level, seeing what the contestants were like when the instructors weren't around. They wanted to know who I'd want by my side if we were going into battle. The contestants would know there was a mole, but not who it was. I knew that this would make them jumpy and prone to accusing every man and his dog of being that mole, so if I was to escape too much suspicion then I'd have to be the grey man, blending into the background.

Obviously I couldn't say I'd just spent a decade in The Regiment, so as my cover story I said that I worked in a double-glazing factory in Preston. This story had two things really going for it. First, I had actually worked in one when I was much younger, so if by chance someone actually knew a bit about double glazing then I wouldn't be caught out by not knowing basic stuff. Second, my time there had been the most boring of my life. There's nothing exciting about double glazing, nothing at all, and every time someone asked me what I did and I told them, I could see their eyes start to glaze over, if you'll excuse the pun. That suited me fine. The less people asked me about myself, the more likely my cover was to survive intact. If I'd said I was a *Mission: Impossible* stunt man or something like that, I'd have been badgered with questions and drawn attention to myself when I needed to do exactly the opposite.

If you're ever in a situation where you need a cover story, make sure you have one as close to the truth as possible. It's those little details that can trip you up, and if you don't have a handle on them then sooner or later you'll get found out. It's the same reason that spies often adopt names with the same initials as their own: it's one less thing to have to remember. If for whatever reason your cover story requires you to have a different birthday than your own, then remember to know what age you should be and also what your star sign should be. Everyone knows both of those about themselves without thinking, and if under questioning you confidently give a fake birth date but then have to say, 'Hold on a sec' while you work out how old you should be or whether you're a Leo or a Capricorn, you'll be busted.

We were filming in Scotland, which was appropriate for two reasons. First, it was the birthplace of David Stirling, who founded the SAS. Second, it's long been a favourite training ground for The Regiment. There aren't many places like it in the world; it's cold, dark and miserable, which makes it a very hard place to operate in. Just the kind of place you want to put people through Selection.

The night before the course started, I went to have dinner with the instructors in their hotel. It was miles away from where the contestants were staying, so I knew there was no danger of being rumbled. We had some lovely steak, drank a couple of decent glasses of wine and had a good old laugh, but I knew the next day when it began for real they wouldn't spare me, and nor should they. Letting me off easy would have been a real giveaway as to my true identity, as would have been beasting me extra hard (though to be honest the latter would have been much harder to pick up on than the former, since the whole point was that everybody would be being pushed to their limits and often beyond).

I got back to the contestants' hotel about midnight. Again, people had come in from flights from all round the country, so everybody had arrived at different times, and my own late arrival wasn't in any way unusual. If anyone asked, I just said I'd got the last flight in from Manchester that night. Besides, it wasn't as if the contestants were all encouraged to get to know each other. The next morning at breakfast we were all instructed to sit on a table on our own if possible rather than start chatting to other people. Obviously the DS can't stop people forming friendships and bonds, but they try to minimise this. The whole point of Selection is that it's an individual thing. It's you against other people, not in tandem with them. It's also you against the course, the instructors and the conditions, but most of all it's you against yourself, which I'll discuss in more detail in 'Resilience'. One of my jobs as mole was to report back as to who was getting close with who, so the DS could try to drive a wedge between them and see what they were made of that way.

We were each given a number on an armband which we had to wear at all times. If you wanted to VW (voluntarily withdraw) you took the armband off: that was the sign you'd quit. The numbers were there so the DS didn't have to keep calling out our names, but of course there was a subtle and deliberate element of dehumanisation here too: you're not a name, you're just a number. I was number four.

There were a lot of personal trainers among the contestants, so I knew there'd be some seriously fit men and women. That didn't bother me. I'd done this for real, which was far tougher. Don't get me wrong, the show replicates Selection as far as it can, and it does a pretty good job, but with the best will in the world it's impossible to mimic it totally or make it as hard as it really is. So I knew my biggest problem would be resisting the urge to show off. Well, not show off as such, but certainly I'd need to dial down my competitiveness. I was supposed to be the grey man, after all, and one sure way of drawing too much attention to myself would be to lead out the field on every single exercise. To some extent when people are being beasted and everyone's absolutely hanging, they don't have the time or energy to look around and gauge who's where in the pecking order, but again it came back to the same thing: don't stand out from the crowd if you don't have to.

This was brought home to me early on when we had to do a hill run. I started at the back and gradually worked my way through the field until I was at the front. When I reached the top of the hill and turned round to see where the others were I realised that the nearest one was 50 metres back!

The next day I was called into the doctor's room as cover so the instructors could talk to me. 'Mate, you've got to be more shit,' thEY said. 'I've heard people talking about you already. And you're using army slang

– redders, threaders, scoff,* that kind of stuff – which people will pick up on sooner or later.' It was a wake-up call: even though I knew what I was supposed to be doing, and should have had the discipline to see that through, I was still fighting against my own competitive fires. I needed to park my ego more. Easier said than done. That ego which made it hard for me to be deliberately shit was the same ego which had got me through P Company, through Selection and to the top of Everest twice: that kernel at the heart of me which would look into someone's eyes and know that I could go longer and faster and better than them. As so often in life, your strengths can sometimes also be your weaknesses.

So I dialled it back a bit, but not so much that, when I would finally be revealed as the mole and join the DS, people wouldn't go, 'Him? *Him*? How the fuck can it be Jay? He's total shit.' In any case, after the first couple of days people were becoming so tired, and so concerned with their own personal performance and chances of making it through, that they started to obsess less over who the mole was. It was a sensible move on their part, even if it wasn't deliberate. The only way to know for sure who the mole was would be when he was revealed. Until then, it was just gossip and using up energy which

---

* Hot, tired and food respectively.

people could ill afford to waste. The identity of the mole wasn't in anyone's list of controllables, so the best thing to do would have been not to worry about it.

Morale started to plummet among the contestants as the days wore on. Part of this, silly as it might sound, was the food. The producers had decided to give us minimal food in both quantity and taste, and it's amazing the effect that has on people. Napoleon said that an army marches on its stomach, and he was damn right.* I just kept my head down and ploughed on. Remember that I knew all the tricks the instructors used. One person's water bottle empty when it should have been full? Everyone gets thrashed. One person dressed incorrectly? Everyone gets thrashed. I knew too that even the most savage beasting doesn't last longer than an hour, so I treated them as basically PT sessions.

The one thing I did want to avoid was failing at the log race, as I knew that whichever group lost that would be forced to stay out that night. You have to carry a massive log over a given distance in a given time, and

* One of the first things I'd clocked on any tour was this: always make friends with the chef. If you do, they give you not just extra rations but the best stuff too. The chef in Lashkar Gah when I was there was an absolutely top man, and he'd come round with lobster tails which he'd saved for us. When you're in hard conditions, something like that is an absolute lifesaver.

you have to do it as a team. People drop off all the time, as it's so hard. I was on the front no matter who was falling off and changing round behind me. My ears were bleeding from carrying the log on my shoulders and swapping sides every now and then to balance out the strain, and I had a rash down my neck, but I didn't care. The wind was blowing in gusts of up to 90mph – in fact, the health and safety boys called the exercise off halfway through as it was so hard for people to keep their own footing, let alone lug a massive log – but I was in my element, yelling at the team leader to get a grip and hammering on through some sort of savage determination. It was almost animalistic.

Later on, to balance that out, I pretended to have trouble putting my harness on when we had to do an exercise with ladders. It was the kind of ham acting which would have shamed a village panto, and I saw one of the instructors turn away so the other contestants wouldn't see him trying not to laugh.

The hardest part for me was the milling. 'Milling' is when you have to get in a boxing ring with someone and hit each other for a minute. The instructors aren't looking for decent boxing techniques and fancy Muhammad Ali shuffle-style footwork. They just want aggression and to see you willing to hurt someone else. I was paired with a contestant called Beth, an art teacher from Cornwall. Beth's sister Ellie was also on the programme, and she and I had become good mates. One of the reasons the DS put me and Beth together was that I'd told them how much Beth and Ellie relied on their mutual support for each other, so this was the DS's way of putting a cat among the pigeons.

I didn't want to mill with Beth, I really didn't. Although everyone was equal on the course and women got no special treatment over the men, I still didn't like the idea of hitting a woman, even one who was a world-class Crossfit practitioner and could lift heavier weights than I could. But you don't get to choose who you mill and you can't refuse to do it, so I just had to get on with it, though I consciously tried not to hit her too hard. When I caught her and she went down onto her knees, Ant yelled 'Keep going!' at me, which was the last thing I wanted; but then Beth got up and caught me with a decent punch that jerked my head back on my neck, so I was glad that she caught me a good one there. After the minute was over we lined up next to each other again and she gave my hand a squeeze to show there were no hard feelings, which reassured me a bit.

But Ellie had been wincing while watching all this, and in the Land Rovers on the way back to the camp Beth was very quiet. When we reached the camp, she started crying. I felt awful, as though this were somehow my fault. 'It's not you,' she said, but I must have looked unconvinced as she started to explain. 'It brought back a lot of things I've really not dealt with,' she said. She'd been in several abusive relationships where guys had beaten her up, and being forced to mill with me hadn't just brought those memories back – it had showed her that she could have, should have, fought back. I gave her a big hug, pretty much on the edge of tears myself. This was the kind of thing which made the programme really useful, I thought: that something like that was actual progress for a real person with a specific problem. I then said to her, 'If you ever want to put gloves on and punch me again, just let me know.'

On the sixth day, we decided it was time for the big reveal. We were doing a surf drill but were told we had to take all our kit, including helmets, and I accidentally-on-purpose forgot mine. We were all jogging on the spot when Ant came up with my helmet in his hand.

'Whose is this?' he yelled.

'Mine, staff,' I replied, doing my best impression of a pupil up before the head teacher.

'Number four, get out here. Look at me. Turn around. Face your fucking muckers. Number four, who are you close to on this course?'

'Number 23, staff.' Number 23 was Ellie.

'Number 23, go and grab your fucking barrel.' This was an old whisky barrel – we were in Scotland, after all. 'Get the barrel above your head. Say, "Thank you, number four."'

This was the kicker. Ellie would be punished for something I'd done: basic collective responsibility stuff. I stared at my feet while Ellie stared at me. Her face was creased in pain from holding the barrel above her head, but the moment she lowered it Ant was into her. 'Get it above your fucking head! I said get it above your head, 23!' I could see Ellie's arms shaking as she unsteadily lifted the barrel above her head.

Eventually – this was all planned, of course – I said, 'Fuck this!', tore off my armband, threw it on the floor and walked away. Ellie shouted 'Don't!', thinking that I was withdrawing because of what she was having to go through, but her microphone chose that moment to malfunction so the drama of the episode was a little bit lost.

'What are you doing, number four?' Ant shouted. He picked up my armband. 'I'm going to give you one opportunity to come back and get this!' But I was gone, and as I turned the corner I heard Ant snarl, 'Fucking anyone else want to follow him?'

A car picked me up and took me back to the hotel: not the contestants' one anymore but the instructors', because I was now officially one of them. I had a hot shower – there are times when even I don't need to be in a wheelie bin full of cold water – had steak with Camembert, and rang my girlfriend. Though I didn't know it, some of the contestants were saying how I'd looked good enough but clearly just didn't have the right mentality.

Two hours later I was back on set, hiding in the wings of the stage. Ant said to the contestants, 'I told you from the beginning that you would be exposed. That we will leave no stone unturned. And that we have eyes and ears everywhere.' That was my cue. I stepped forward so they could all see me. I heard a few gasps, subdued because they were on parade and knew by now to tone down their normal reactions, and a couple of guys gave me nods of respect for having fooled them so thoroughly. Most of all, I was happy for Ellie, who now knew that I hadn't VW'ed because of her.

'Let me introduce you to someone you knew as Jamie,' Ant continued. 'But fucking no more. He was one of us. From now on you will address him as "staff" at all times. We know absolutely everything about every single one of you.'

I did the last four days as an instructor, and was pretty impressed with how well some of the contestants did. Like I said, it wasn't an exact replica of Selection, but by the same token the contestants weren't full-time soldiers either.

SAS: Who Dares Wins was a great opportunity for me, but that was all it was. Again, I never considered that I would be doing this for a long time and I will not be back for the next series.

LEADERSHIP

> Leadership is the art of getting someone else to do
> something you want done because he wants to do it.
> **Dwight D. Eisenhower**

I've served under both types of leader, good and bad –
actually, I've served under great ones and awful ones
– and in either case the results cascade all the way down
the ranks and affect pretty much every aspect of life.
Few things make as much difference to people as leadership. This difference can be either positive or negative,
and believe me you know the difference.

On my first tour of Afghanistan in 2006, my sergeant
was Dan Jarvie. He was an absolute legend: a big Scot
with a booming voice which you could hear coming a
mile off and a handshake which could crush iron rail-
ings. He was firm, he was decisive and he had high

standards. If you fell short of them, then fuck me he let you know about it. But he never asked anything of you that he wouldn't do himself. He was inspirational, and most of all he always let you know that he had your back. His men all loved him, and he was a big part of why that tour remains one of my fondest memories of my time in the army.

'Alreet, mate?' he'd always ask, but unlike most people he actually wanted to know the answer. Whatever decisions he made, he considered everyone in them, down to the lowliest grunt. When we arrived in Afghanistan, Camp Bastion – the HQ for all British forces there – hadn't really been set up yet. It was just a dustbowl with rows of green 6 × 9 tents and rough tracks flattened by rollers. We ate out of ten-man ration packs – the kitchen and canteen weren't even in operation – and there wasn't even a physical perimeter: no barbed wire, let alone proper Hesco walls. You could see anyone coming a mile off – that was why Bastion was sited where it was – but it was still a little weird just having manned posts in a 360 arc as your only line of security. It's easy to slot in somewhere when it's all up and running properly, with systems in place and everyone knowing what they're doing, but when you're coming into a place which is still very much under construction it's absolutely imperative that the leader creates not just a unit but a team, a family. Dan did that.

The flipside was another sergeant I had, who obviously I won't name. I won't even say at what stage of my career it was at, so as not to identify him, but trust me, everyone who served with me under him felt the same way I did. He was pretty much every way Dan's exact opposite. He was one of those people who, having got to a position of power, now forgot the skills which had got him there: the nuances, the myriad little bits of how to manage. He'd come up through the ranks and should have remembered that, because it would have kept him grounded and connected to the people he was in charge of, but he didn't. Power had got to him and made him think he was something he wasn't.

It would have been bad enough if he'd been a good leader who was just a bit overbearing, but he was anything but. He was weak and lacked confidence in himself, which he chose to deal with by projecting it onto us, his men: micromanaging and not trusting us to do our jobs, blaming us for things that were his fault and always acting paranoid that we disliked him. We did dislike him, of course – as the old saying goes, it's not paranoid if they really are out to get you – but it was a vicious circle. Whenever we tried to raise an issue which he thought reflected badly on him, he'd just lash out and blame us, making it impossible to have a proper conversation and sort out some of the problems. He was more concerned with what his superiors thought than what his men thought, which is always the kiss of death for any leader. I and some others tried to tell him that his superiors would think well of him if his men did, because that would mean he was doing a good job, but he couldn't or wouldn't see that. I was reminded that some soldiers in Vietnam had 'fragged' their superior officers – that is, killed them with fragmentation grenades in the heat of battle and blamed it on the enemy. Obviously this never got anywhere near that stage, and I would never have wished such a fate on him (or anybody), but what it showed was the need to look out for the collective. A bad leader doesn't just affect himself: he affects every person around him.

And as a leader, it's all about people, first and last. A good leader makes for happy people, and happy people make for a good team. The Roman emperor Caligula famously said, '*Oderint dum metuant*' – 'Let them hate, so long as they fear' – but that's not a recipe for good leadership, certainly not in the long term. If people only do what you tell them to because they're scared of you, then they'll only do what you tell them for as long as they're scared of you. One day that fear will go, or you'll realise that things are now so bad that you haven't got much left to lose. Either way, the leader loses everything when that moment comes. In contrast, a leader who makes his men happy empowers them to keep going on their own accord rather than just his own. Treat them with respect and listen to what they want, and not only will you keep them happy, but you'll also improve the performance of your team, which is – or should be – your ultimate aim.

It sounds simple when put this way, but of course if it was that easy then anyone could do it. Leadership is difficult for lots of reasons, but the base one is this: everyone is different, and so the practice and methods of leadership are always varying. Leaders are different. Followers are different. Peers are different. Former Navy SEAL Jocko Willink says, 'What makes leadership so hard is dealing with people, and people are crazy. And the craziest person a leader has to deal with is themselves.'

Perhaps above all else, a leader must be balanced. Again, this is easier said than done, because it's easy for a strength to become a weakness or a positive to become a negative. It's like the points in 'Opportunity' about looking so hard for openings that you fail to assess them properly, or about the drive and determination which had helped me achieve so much risking blowing my cover as the mole on *Who Dares Wins* because I couldn't keep my ego in check. When you're used to a personal quality or characteristic being a strength, it's hard to judge the point at which it becomes a weakness. The leader constantly has to deal with forces and issues which are pulling him in different and often contradictory directions at the same time. Willink again: 'Leaders must talk, but if they talk too much, they overwhelm their subordinates with information. On the other hand, if they talk too little, the troops aren't properly informed. A leader must be aggressive, but if they are too aggressive they might expose themselves to unnecessary risk. Contrarily, if they are not aggressive enough they will never make progress. This list of dichotomies goes on indefinitely.'

They say that kids never forget the teachers who inspired them, and the same applies to soldiers about leaders. Vice-Admiral Cuthbert Collingwood, who was Horatio Nelson's second-in-command at the Battle of Trafalgar in 1805 and is buried alongside him in St Paul's Cathedral, is a good example. At a time when many admirals ruled their charges by fear, Collingwood was different. He had no time for either press ganging or flogging, and his men loved him. A sailor who served under him wrote that 'He and his dog Bounce were known to every member of the crew. How attentive he was to the health and comfort and happiness of his crew! A man who could not be happy under him could have been happy nowhere; a look of displeasure from him was as bad as a dozen at the gangway from another man. A better seaman, a better friend to seamen, a more zealous defender of the country's rights and honour, never trod the quarterdeck.'

So too General William Garrison, who commanded US forces in the 1993 Battle of Mogadishu (later filmed as *Black Hawk Down*). One of the soldiers who fought that day described Garrison as 'the finest general officer I have ever worked for and probably ever will. He understood his men and how we thought, what we wanted and needed, and understood the situation anywhere he was, immediately and completely. He is the finest leader an operator could ask for.'

My own personal role model was Bryan Budd, with whom I served in 3 Para and who was killed on that 2006 tour. He was always the same, always totally genuine, in and out of contact. Rounds would be cracking off all around and he'd be on the net calm as you like, as though he was putting the cat out for the night. He used to put pictures of his family up around his bed, and was totally unashamed of saying how much he loved them. He seemed indestructible, which made me and all the other lads believe in him 100 per cent. Dan Jarvie called him 'outrageously fit, outrageously switched on, with a mega sense of humour and very, very helpful'.

One day we were getting mortared and pretty much everyone did the sensible thing and went down to the basement to wait it out. Our platoon commander, said: 'I decided to go up to the top of the tower to see where the mortars were coming from and call in air support if need be. But who was there, already doing exactly what I was going to? Bryan Budd. That was typical. He thought above and beyond his immediate safety and about the bigger picture. He would always be happy to go forward. There would never be any questions, any indications that he was scared and didn't want to do it.'

Even after he died I used to talk to him in my head, asking for his advice on what to do in certain situations. I wanted to be like him. I felt like Luke Skywalker asking Obi-Wan Kenobi to teach him how to use the Force. Trust me, when you're a leader you want someone to look at you the same way I looked at Bryan Budd. And if you're doing your job properly, then they will.

Leadership for me is all about looking and being aware, and there are six categories of this: look in and look out, look up and look down, look forward and look back.

LOOK IN

Being a leader is all about managing other people. But, perhaps counterintuitively, as a leader you have to keep constantly checking in on yourself. There was an army advert a few years ago showing a bunch of soldiers delivering food and water to starving and thirsty refugees. The crowd was agitated and the soldiers had to keep order. 'Who do you supply first?' asked a caption. The answer was the soldiers themselves: they can't do their job if they haven't had enough food and water. The same principle applies in an aircraft if cabin pressure fails: always fix your oxygen mask first before helping someone else with theirs. It's not selfish: it's ensuring that you can be as effective as possible for everyone around you.

You have so many more responsibilities than your subordinates, and these can eat up your time and your focus, making it easy to find your own performance levels slipping. It often happens in sport too. Cricketers see their batting average drop during their periods of captaincy. Tour de France leaders have to spend hours each day fulfilling media and sponsorship obligations while team-mates and rivals alike are resting and recovering. You can spend so much time looking out for and after other people that you forget to give yourself the same levels of care. Ah well, you can say, that's my job, to look after other people. Yes, it is; but the core of your job is also still what it was before you became the leader.

So you can't afford to let such performance drops happen to you. A soldier in any form of leadership role – a commanding officer, a platoon sergeant, a troop leader – can't afford to slack on fitness, or weapons drills, or tactical awareness, or any of the many other things he rightly demands from his men. You need to maintain your own performance levels, not just for the group's sake – they can't afford to be carrying a passenger – but for your own too. If you're not pulling your weight in your own personal tasks, that will be immediately noticed, seized upon and dissected, and you'll begin to lose respect from the others, no matter how well you're performing your leadership duties themselves.

So you need to know when to be selfish. One of the paradoxes of leadership is this: sometimes the best way, maybe the only way, of being a selfless leader is to be selfish. For example, you have to prioritise. When there are lots of competing demands on your time, assess each of them according to two criteria: importance and urgency. It's a simple 2 × 2 matrix. If something's important but doesn't need doing now, don't do it. If something needs doing now but isn't important, don't do it. If something's neither important nor urgent, definitely don't do it! Only if something's both important and urgent should you do it.

Knowing how to judge whether something meets both these criteria is a skill in itself, as is the nature of what to do about it. Say a squadron leader is approached by one of his men who confides that he's having marriage problems.* How should he deal with it best? First he needs to ascertain whether this is affecting or likely to affect the soldier's performance. If it's not, then the leader might decide with the best will in the world that this is not his problem. But if it is liable to become an issue at work, then it's very much the leader's problem right there. Performance in the army is very literally a matter of life and death sometimes, and you can't take any chances with that. If it is going to affect that performance, then by definition it's both important and urgent.

So the leader needs to deal with it. But this may not necessarily be a job for the leader himself. He needs to decide what the soldier in question actually needs. Does he need a marriage counsellor, because he's trying to

---

* Trust me, this is hardly uncommon in the army. At least, the problems are hardly uncommon. The confiding happens a little less often.

save his marriage? Does he need a therapist to help him work through some of his own personal issues which might be contributing to those marriage problems? Does he need a night getting hammered with his best mate in the squadron? He might need all three. But none of them actually involve the leader spending time that he'll find difficult to spare in an area which is not necessarily his own expertise – in which, in fact, he risks doing more harm than good unless he's careful. Passing responsibility off onto others in such instances isn't weakness or a dereliction of duty: it's sensible delegation which will maximise the performance both of the leader and the man who came to him in the first place.

Looking in also involves examining your own personality and checking that you're up to the task. You may doubt that you are, which is not necessarily a bad thing. Beware the man who never doubts himself and thinks he knows everything about everything. As discussed earlier, a little bit of impostor syndrome keeps you sharp and humble, and humility is never a bad thing in a leader. There's a reason why David Stirling put it at the heart of the SAS ethos. Humility is the quality a leader needs above all else, as a leader who lacks humility won't acknowledge his own weaknesses, and therefore will never act to counterbalance the areas in which he's not so strong, and therefore will never improve either himself or his team. As ever, of course, balance is crucial here. Constantly doubting and second-guessing yourself to the extent that you can't even decide what to have for breakfast might be good if you're playing Hamlet, but it's pretty shit if you're trying to be a leader.

A leader needs to be working harder than anyone else on the team. No job should be beneath or beyond them. They need to have integrity and honesty, and not to say anything behind someone's back that they wouldn't say to their face. They need to subdue their own ego to the success and cohesion of the unit. A true leader can never be anything other than a genuine person, especially in the military. Soldiers have a lower tolerance for bullshit than pretty much any other group of people in society, and we can spot fakes five miles away in a high wind. And once someone's been pegged as a fake, it's very hard for them to come back from that.

LOOK OUT

'Look out' can have two separate but equally important meanings: look outwards from yourself towards the people under your command, and look out for dangers and pitfalls which will require your attention. This section will cover the first of those; the second is discussed in 'look forward' later in the chapter.

The people who you're leading are the most important aspects of your job, and if they're not then you're doing it wrong. You have to look out for them both on a group level and also as individuals. Any group – a military unit, a rugby team, a corporate department – is a collective, but everyone within that collective is an individual. Those individuals are very different from each other. Each person has their own strengths and weaknesses, their own hopes and fears, their own areas of confidence and insecurity. In the 1991 World Rowing Championships, the British men's eight was coxed by Garry Herbert. As the crew began their final sprint for home in the final, he began to go down the boat calling out to each man in turn, reminding them of their individual motivations: the man who wanted to make his kids proud, the man whose parents had sacrificed so much to drive him around to training and competitions as a kid, the man whose teacher had told him he'd never amount to much. They won a bronze medal they'd never expected to be in the mix for, and much of that was down to Herbert and his ability to switch on to the needs of his crew.

Being able to get the best out of people is key to being a leader. Some people need a kick up the arse every now and then; others need an arm round the shoulder. Knowing which is which is crucial. Get it wrong and you can do more harm than good.

But you can only do this if you know people. You don't have to be everyone's best mate or remember the name of their wife's hairdresser's second cousin, but you *do* need to know what's important in their lives: what's going on at home, which football team they support, what they like to do at weekends. If things are good outside work then they're more likely to be good at work; if they're not then the opposite applies. When a Maasai warrior is sick, his peers ask him, 'Who have you been arguing with?' The question isn't a literal one, or at least not only a literal one. Rather, it's designed to find which part of his life is out of whack, because the Maasai see something which we in the West can forget: we are all part of our environment. Everything plays on everything else. An 'argument' can be a sick cow, or a drought on crops, or anything which means that things aren't going smoothly.

No one can keep their home and work lives inseparable, not for ever. And when you work for an organisation such as the army which has clout and resources, you can use them to help not just your employees but their dependants too: someone to go with a soldier's wife to a scan if he's deployed overseas, or to provide emergency childcare for their kids, or go and sit with an elderly and maybe lonely widowed parent. As a leader you demand a lot of time from your people, but sometimes leadership is about giving people time rather than taking it from them. And people remember this. Say you lose them for a day or two, even for a week or two. Further down the line, they'll remember the kindness and sympathy you showed and will work even harder for you.

As leader, you have to be as available and inclusive as possible. If you come into a canteen and see three tables full of people, which one do you sit at? The smart leader goes to the one where he knows fewest of those people well. It lets him get to know them better, which in turn allows him to help them more. It means they'll be more likely to come to him with a problem or a suggestion. And it nixes any perception that he might think himself better than them or be part of a clique with his own favourites. Of course you get on better with some people than with others – that's just human nature – but as leader you can't be seen to be hanging around with just the same people all the time. Groups are very sensitive to who's 'in' and who's 'out', who has access to and influence on the powerful ones and who doesn't. A good leader has to ensure that no one feels marginalised.

Being sensitive to individuals' needs also extends to the needs of the collective as a whole. When we came back from the 2006 tour we had one last night together where we all got absolutely wasted and ended up punching some windows out. The next morning the platoon sergeant turned up, took a look at the damage and said simply: 'Just get 'em replaced by the end of today.' He understood that we hadn't been just smashing things up for the sake of mindless violence: we'd just come back from six months in a war zone where we'd been in scraps pretty much every day, and we had a lot of energy and emotion to get out of our systems. The sergeant was able to access his humanity when it was necessary, and that's an invaluable leadership skill. Situations are fluid, people's moods and circumstances are fluid, and by looking out both for and towards his men a good leader will be able to be flexible within certain parameters. If people say they're tired and want a rest, are they just being lazy or do they feel it would be beneficial in the long run? You can't answer this question without knowing your men well enough to understand their baseline moods. If guys who normally work hard and are committed to their jobs say they need to ease back, then listen carefully. A habitual skiver who says the same may get rather shorter shrift …

This also allows you to instil a culture of honesty throughout your unit, and honesty is absolutely key. A good leader owns his mistakes and doesn't make excuses, and in doing so not so much encourages as demands that his men do the same. When other people see you being honest, it inspires them to follow suit. If everyone in a team does that, the environment is healthy and the team has the best chance of improving and performing well. Don't worry about making mistakes. No one's perfect. Everyone makes mistakes. The only way not to make a mistake is not to try something in the first place. Making a mistake isn't wrong or unprofessional. What *is* wrong and unprofessional is trying to sweep that mistake under the carpet, because by pretending it never happened you deny yourself the opportunity to learn from it next time round.

Most leaders, certainly in the army, like to hold debriefing sessions where everyone can be honest about everything – their own performance and everyone else's too. The difference between a good leader and a poor one is that a good leader means what he says when he talks about people being honest in these situations. A bad leader only means it up to the point where someone criticises him, at which point he deflects blame or just stops listening and renders the whole thing pointless. The whole purpose of a no-holds-barred debrief is that everybody is trying to improve the collective's performance, not settle personal scores or criticise other people for the sake of it. If people are pulling their punches then there's no point. The leader's job is to ensure the improvement without letting the session deteriorate into a slanging match, but to do that he has to be prepared to cop flak coming his way on the chin too rather than just expect everyone else but him to do so. If that criticism's accurate, then he should accept and address it; if it's not, then he should explain why.

LOOK UP

A leader should always make time to look up. I don't mean in terms of casting an eye towards the ranks above him, to check that he's gaining their approval; quite the opposite. A leader who does this, like the bad sergeant I spoke about at the start of the chapter, has his priorities all to cock. It's simple input–output: if your input (being a good leader to those below you) is good, then your output (impressing those above you) will almost always look after itself.

No, by looking up I mean two things. First, continuing to set goals for improvement, both your own personal improvement and that of your team. Second, keeping the mood of the collective up by introducing and maintaining a culture of positivity.

No leader is perfect, no matter how good they think they are. Every leader always has room for improvement, no matter how minuscule they feel that improvement may be. Accepting the first and pursuing the second come down to the same thing: persistence.

You don't just become a leader and instantly know everything there is to know about it. Leadership is a process, not an event. You learn on the job, and you never stop learning: even the most experienced and successful leader has gaps in their knowledge and a skillset which can be plugged.

The ranking system in the army is a good indication of this. As you climb the ranks, you find yourself being given gradually more and more responsibility. At every turn you're becoming a better leader, if you're doing it right, but you're also coming up against the limitations of your own experience. You can see this pattern in soldier and officer ranks alike:

- A soldier's first taste of leadership comes as *Lance Corporal*, who supervises a section (a small team of up to four soldiers).
- Next – and, as for all these promotions, always assuming the soldier has demonstrated a proven ability to lead – comes a *Corporal*, who is given command of more soldiers and equipment such as tanks and guns.
- The following step up is to *Sergeant*, who is typically a second-in-command of a troop or platoon of up to 35 soldiers, and has responsibility for advising and assisting junior officers.

- Then comes *Staff Sergeant*, combining man and resource management of around 120 soldiers or even command of a platoon or troop.

The two most senior soldier ranks beyond this are those of Warrant Officer:

- *Warrant Officer Class 2* focuses on the training, welfare and discipline of a company, squadron or battery of up to 120 soldiers. A WO2 also acts as a senior advisor to the Major in command of the sub-unit and may be selected for commission as an officer.
- *Warrant Officer Class 1*, typically reached after 18 years of outstanding service, is the senior advisor of their unit's commanding officer, with leadership, discipline and welfare responsibilities of up to 650 officers and soldiers, as well as equipment.

At each stage of promotion the leader is given more responsibility in three areas: the number of men for whom he's responsible, the amount of resources under his management, and the extent of liaison with and advice to officers. A leader who keeps looking up should both aspire to the next level of seniority (if that fits his personality and career/life plans, of course), while being conscious of what he still needs to do to get there and determined to accomplish those tasks in order to make him a good candidate for promotion. Wanting too much responsibility too soon is in its own way as damaging as shying away from progression through fear or laziness: you can look up too far as well as not far enough.

The officer ranks follow a similar pattern of increasing responsibility for men, resources and extra roles:

- *Second Lieutenant*, the rank held on commission from Sandhurst, is responsible for leading up to 30 soldiers in a platoon or troop, both in training and on operations.
- *Lieutenant* is a small step up from here, and then comes *Captain*, normally second-in-command of a sub-unit of up to 120 soldiers and with tactical responsibility for operations on the ground as well as equipment maintenance, logistic support and manpower.
- That sub-unit is under the charge of a *Major*, who has responsibility for those soldiers' training, welfare and administration.
- Above the Major is the *Lieutenant Colonel*, who commands a unit of up to 650 soldiers, and above the Lieutenant Colonel is the *Colonel*, who serves as a staff officer between field commands at battalion

or brigade level and is the principal advisor to one or more senior officers.

- Then comes a *Brigadier*, who can command a brigade or be a director of operational capability groups such as a director of staff.
- Next are the *Major-General* (two-star), who commands a division and holds a senior staff appointment in the MOD; the *Lieutenant-General* (three-star), who commands a corps and holds a very senior MOD staff appointment; and finally the *General* (four-star), who holds one of the most senior appointments such as Chief of Defence Staff, Chief of the General Staff, or similar.*

Any decent leader who's made their way up these ladders has by definition kept looking up and kept on at making themselves a better leader, through all the times they've doubted themselves, until perhaps they finally feel that they're worth the role they perhaps hadn't felt themselves worth when they'd first been given it. Persistence as a leader involves constant self-questioning. If you do something well, can you do it even better? If you don't do something so well, how can you improve that? As I said, the process never ends;

* Field Marshal is above all these but is an honorary rank.

or if it does, it's because the leader has come up against the Peter Principle, where he is promoted to a level at which he proves incompetent and therefore makes no further progress, which in turn means by definition that he's not a good leader.

The second part of looking up is positivity, and this is also connected to improvement. Being positive is about setting standards, not limits. It takes no more energy to have a bigger goal than a smaller one. So the positive leader is at an advantage here.

It's obvious that radiators make better leaders than drains, and part of being a radiator is feeling positive and making sure that spreads to other people. There's not much point being positive unless you transmit that positivity to the team. In army terms, someone might find it easy to gee people up when things are hairy and the bullets are flying, but in downtime they could be too quiet and too reserved, so many of the good things they're feeling don't really come across.

If this is the case, the leader has to talk more, to make sure that his men know he's feeling good about himself and them too. A positive leader will do things like ask each man for things he likes about his comrades and then make sure that the praise is relayed back, not in a cheesy or embarrassing way but in a way that lets people know that they're valued by those they're standing and fighting alongside. Positive affirmation is important. People in general respond better to positivity than to negativity, to being reinforced rather than undermined. A positive team is more likely to be a confident team; a confident team is more likely to be a successful one. A leader's job is to do his best to ensure that.

But equally there are plenty of times when even the most dynamic and upbeat person doesn't feel that positive. When that's the case, the good leader should try to keep his negativity to himself, or share it only with a very few people whom he trusts and get them to help him work it out. In a team environment, both positivity and negativity emanate more from the person at the top than from any other single person, and they're both contagious. Positivity's worth catching. Negativity isn't.

LOOK DOWN

Organisations are hierarchies. They are structured around systems and networks which more often than not are vertical rather than horizontal; that is, people are layered according to seniority and responsibility, and report up and down the chain rather than across it. This is how human society has been organised pretty much since the earliest days of civilisation, for good reasons (experience, accountability, clarity of leadership) and bad (power, corruption and nepotism) alike, and whether the leader agrees with it or not is beside the point. The leader has to work with the world as it is, not as he would like it to be.

But one of the things which vertical hierarchies do is equate value with seniority. The nearer the top an individual gets, the more their contribution is valued, both in terms of influence but also of course remuneration. A major-general is not only paid more than a sergeant, for example, but more people listen when he speaks, he has access to far more by way of resources, and so on. In any number of ways, a major-general is seen as more important than a sergeant.

The good leader, the leader who looks down, doesn't think so.

A leader has to look down because that's the nature of the organisation he's working in. But he's not looking down in the sense of being disdainful. He's looking down because he understands that every person for whom he has responsibility is a vital part of the machine. As the famous US General George S. Patton said: 'Every single man in this army plays a vital role. Don't ever let up. Don't ever think that your job is unimportant. Every man has a job to do and he must do it. Every man is a vital link in the great chain.'

A bad leader ignores that advice, and as a result people without authority feel scared or disinclined to speak up, for fear that they won't be listened to or even be punished for doing so. A mediocre leader pays lip service to that advice, and though he may talk a good game, the results – or lack of them – tell otherwise: people might feel it's OK to stand up, but they soon stop trying if nothing ever comes of it. A good leader not only believes that advice but also acts on it. A good leader knows that rank is not in itself a reflection of value. The most experienced general in the army can have a terrible idea; the lowliest private can come up with something which is total genius; a cleaning lady can stumble across a vital piece of information or intelligence. An idea's value comes from its own merits or demerits, not from the standing of the person who said it. Only by looking down at all your men, by encouraging them to speak up and by affirming the importance of their roles, do you empower them to be as good as they can be.

Take a standard army patrol. Which member is the most important? It's the point man who leads the line, watches for ambushes, booby traps and IEDs, and will be first into contact if the enemy are engaged and the bullets start flying. No, it's the guy with the radio on his back who's the patrol's link to base and who can get on the net to call for air cover, casualty evacuations or infantry reinforcement when needed. No, it's the medic whose skill and calmness under pressure will keep blokes alive even when they've suffered injuries so bad that even five years ago, certainly ten, they'd probably have bled out on the battlefield. No, it's the machine gunner at the back who'll lay down suppressive fire if they get into a contact and allow everyone else to take up the best positions possible while he sprays and prays. No, it's the leader himself who has to knit all these disparate elements together. And on, and on, and on.

The answer, of course, is that everyone's important, irrespective of their role. This is as true in the civilian world as it is in the military. Take a film set, for example. Who's the most important person on a film set? The director, because it's his vision for the movie which will determine its success or failure? The producer, without whom there'd be no financing, no permissions to shoot and no contracts for the crew? The writer, because before any of these scores of people were here the film was just a blank page on his laptop? The actors, who can make a good script bad or a bad script good? The cameramen who have to shoot the action, otherwise it's just going to be a radio play? The sound guys, without whom this would be a silent movie? The set designers, because the look of a set is so important to the tone of the movie and otherwise you might as well just shoot it in a white room? The make-up and costume departments who make the actors look the way they're supposed to? The special effects guys? The security personnel who have to stop members of the public wandering in? The caterers?* Again, as with the patrol, it's all of them. Everyone's job is mission critical (and if it's not then they shouldn't be there), and if anyone fails at their job then the effects can be severe.

The leader who looks down neutralises the effect of rank and position. This is one of the reasons that the UK Special Forces have been and continue to be so effective: we basically do away with rank. The moment you join UKSF, you revert to the rank of trooper (private) if you're enlisted, or you're demoted to your previous rank if you're an officer. If either of those bother you, you're in the wrong place. There are still ranks in the Special Forces, but they're much, much less important than in the Green Army. The Special Forces not only want but actively require thinking soldiers, blokes who won't just automatically do what they're told but who'll be prepared to argue the toss in an effort to make anything – a plan, an exercise, even a night out

* Actually, most people who've been on a film set would say that the caterers are indeed the most important people there. See Napoleon's point about an army marching on its stomach.

– better than it was originally scheduled to be. When you're Tier One operators, performing some of the most skilful and riskiest military operations there are, you have to be able to think on your feet and take responsibility at all times and in all circumstances. As a result, everybody in the Special Forces is expected to be both a leader and a team player, and everybody is seen as being on the same level as everyone else. And if everyone feels they've had input into a plan, they're more likely to carry it out to the best of their ability than if they feel it's been imposed on them without proper consultation.

When Louis, Staz and I – all former SF operators – began ThruDark, we applied the same principles. We picked people on personality rather than experience. What we cared about most was that they had the raw materials: that they'd fit in, work hard and show initiative. The job itself we could teach them and they could learn: that wasn't the issue. We didn't care what someone had done before joining us; we cared what they could do once they'd joined us. One guy turned up for an interview in a pink collared shirt and tie. We were in T-shirts and shorts, and we were like, mate, this is an outdoor clothing company who need you to run support and liaise with delivery companies. It's not a merchant bank. Needless to say, he didn't get the job. His CV had looked decent, which was why we'd interviewed him, but the moment he walked through the door I knew he'd be all wrong.

In fact, if it was up to me I'd abolish CVs altogether. A good leader has no need for them, no need at all. They just encourage people to try to make a season captaining their second XI hockey sound like they've won Olympic gold. They're pretty much non-stop exercises in bullshit. To my mind, *The Spectator* magazine has it exactly right. This is how they advertise for interns (who are paid, unlike in many companies):

> We don't ask for CVs: we don't care where (or whether) you went to university. When we judge applications we don't even look at names: our HR department takes them out. Exams are a snapshot of how things were going for you at a certain point in your teenage years which is why CVs are of limited use. You might be one of Lord Rothermere's relatives, you might be a 35-year-old shelf-stacker. We don't care and we don't ask. All that matters is flair, enthusiasm and capacity for hard work.

For a leader who still has to work within a hierarchy, it's not the actual elimination of rank which is important here; it's the effect that elimination has. Treat everybody the same, listen to everyone's input, and looking down will pay huge dividends not just for the leader but more importantly for the team too. A leader who feels threatened by those beneath him will hoard responsibility and power; a leader genuinely concerned for the team welfare will delegate and give people roles. Any leader who wants to take everything on themselves and not trust anybody else to do anything is harming the team and making it all about himself, in which case he shouldn't be leader in the first place.

No leader can do it all himself. It doesn't matter how experienced they are, how intelligent, how prepared or how committed. Every leader needs input from other people to allow them to make the best decisions possible. They need perspective, and they can only get that perspective by consulting others. These others won't just give the leader good advice; they'll give him fresh and interesting viewpoints too, because their personalities, their experiences and their areas of expertise will be different not just from the leader's but from each other's too.

Doing away with rank also helps the leader put away his ego, as discussed in 'Look In'. A leader who can listen to an alternative plan from the one he proposed and admit that it's better is not a weak leader ceding ground to an underling; he's a strong leader with the self-confidence to take different ideas on board. As Harry Truman, US president and once an army colonel, said: 'It's amazing what you can accomplish if you don't care who gets the credit.'

LOOK FORWARD

A good leader doesn't just look at what's immediately in front of him, but what's in the future too. No organisation is static – if it is, it's not going to survive very long – and the leader must not just be prepared for change but actively welcome it.

It's often said about armies that they're very good at fighting the last war. Human nature more often than not is to cling to something which has been tried and tested, and even more so if this has brought demonstrable success. Those who would break the mould and disrupt the established way of doing things are often dismissed as cranks, belittled or marginalised; but among the eccentric lunatics are often genuine visionaries. A leader who is one of these visionaries, or at least who knows where to find one, has a great advantage over someone hidebound by being confined to the same old same old.

Look at how much warfare has changed in the past century. If you were to take a British Tommy from the Somme in the First World War, whose main experience of warfare had been foul, sodden, stinking, disease-ridden trenches, and plonk him down in the command centre of modern-day armed forces, he'd probably keel over in shock. Supersonic fighter jets, nuclear submarines capable of being submerged for three months or so, drones delivering computer-guided missiles capable of destroying subterranean structures several storeys deep, massive aircraft carriers, and perhaps most of all the kind of cyberwarfare capacities which see a computer virus disable the Iranian nuclear centrifuges.

Now imagine what warfare will look like in another 100 years' time. In many ways that's as impossible to envisage as today's conditions would have been to the First World War Tommy; it's hard to imagine things that don't even exist yet. But a good leader has to try – maybe not to imagine something so far in the future that he won't be around to see it, but certainly some of the earliest stepping stones on the road to that future, the kind he will be around not just to witness but also experience and be affected by.

A leader has to keep his eye on the kind of changes likely to affect him and his team at both a macro and a micro level. Macro factors include political, technological, social and environmental changes. Even as far back as the 1980s, for example, Shell were examining divorce rates in China to try and extrapolate what

Chinese energy demands would be several decades hence if more households were living apart than together. Clearly Shell knew they wouldn't be able to predict these things accurately, but even ballpark figures help in terms of resource planning.

Take the coronavirus pandemic, which has been as serious a test of leadership for prime ministers and presidents around the world as any in recent memory. It's often said that the virus was unprecedented and that no country could have prepared properly for it. To an extent this is true, but there had also been plenty of warnings from scientific and other bodies about not just the likelihood of a pandemic but also the devastating effects of one. Some countries prepared better than others. They didn't think that they could do everything to combat the virus, but they did think – quite correctly – that it was better to do something than nothing. A leader who looks forward may not be able to totally control events, but he will be able at least to respond to them better than those who haven't and are playing catch-up.

There are many events which are less dramatic than worldwide pandemics but which will have effects which are just as important, if not more so. A corporate leader will have to look forward to developments in automation, for example. Many blue-collar jobs have already been superseded by automation, and increasingly some white-collar jobs are going the same way; it might not be too long until some lawyers and doctors are replaced by their virtual counterparts, for example. This might be bad news for those who will lose their jobs, but the employment market is no less fluid than any other part of society, and change will create new jobs just as surely as it wipes out some old ones.

This kind of area is where macro bleeds through to micro: the actual people for whom the leader is responsible. Those people will change too. Indeed, a good leader will often find that their own skill ensures a turnover of staff as those who've benefited from his leadership make progress of their own. One of the reasons my 2008 tour of Afghanistan wasn't as enjoyable as the one two years before was that the personnel weren't the same, and that some of the real quality boys had moved on – a few of them to Hereford and The Regiment. That was partly down to the brilliant leadership we'd received, which had encouraged us to be the best soldiers we could be and had stood those who'd gone on Selection in good stead.

Wayne Gretzky, probably the greatest ice-hockey player in history, was once asked the secret of his success. He explained that he wasn't the quickest player, or the strongest, or the best skater. What really made him good was the advice his dad had given him as a young boy: 'Don't skate to where the puck is. Skate to where the puck will be.' It was Gretzky's anticipation which set him apart from everyone else. That's the kind of forward-looking attitude a good leader needs to cultivate. The future is not something that just happens: we're constantly creating it by our decisions and actions. Change is constant and inevitable, and those who resist it seldom succeed.

LOOK BACK

Looking back sounds like a negative thing: a hankering after the past, a reaction against change, even a fear of the future. But in the hands of a good leader, looking back need be none of these things.

For a start, what happened in the past can provide valuable lessons for the leader going forward. You can't change what's already happened, but you can analyse it, build on it and learn from it. This applies whether what's happened has been a success or a failure. It's often said that you learn more from failures than successes, but a good leader will examine them in just the same way, just as Rudyard Kipling exhorted the readers of 'If' to treat the twin impostors of triumph and disaster just the same.

Whether something has been a success or a failure is not the only thing which defines it. A success can be fluky and in practical terms undeserved; a failure can be unlucky. The Battle of Agincourt in 1415 might have turned out very differently if it hadn't rained so heavily beforehand. The French had planned to use the narrowness of the battlefield to their advantage, but instead they found themselves sinking in the mud, which was even harder in full plate armour, which meant that they were exhausted by the time they reached the English lines, which meant that many fell and drowned in the mud, which made it harder for those behind them to manoeuvre: a litany of woes which all began with heavy rainfall. On a dry day, who knows what would have happened? It's tempting to think that the result is the be-all and end-all, and in some way preordained. That can simply not be true. The good leader looks beyond the result and assesses the processes and events which led up to that result. What went well? What could have been done better? What should we do next time?

Looking back has another meaning too. Leaders are often exhorted to lead from the front – set the example, be first into danger, not ask their men to do anything they wouldn't do themselves. And there are plenty of circumstances, especially in the military, where this is very much the case. But the flipside is that a leader who insists on going first no matter what the situation may be putting himself at unnecessary risk, and even if he doesn't he may be so caught up in the immediate situation in front of him that he can't get an appreciation of the bigger picture.

Sometimes, therefore, it's better for the leader to be at the back: leading from the rear and scanning the entire arena. This applies not just in the thick of the action but in the decision-making process which has led up to it too. A leader confident enough to hang back won't present his men with a plan – he'll let them work one out for themselves. Sure, he'll give input if he feels that the process needs a nudge on the tiller, and if there's deadlock between two opposing points of view then he'll make a decision as to which way to go, but in essence the less visible he can be the better. Too many people in too many walks of life feel that they constantly need to justify themselves – their jobs, their status, their very existence – by not only doing things but being seen to do things. It takes a rare, wise and confident leader to look at a plan and say, 'This is great. You guys crack on.'

There's a well-known internet meme which shows a wolf pack moving through a snowy landscape. The caption goes something like this. 'A wolf pack. The first three are the old or sick: they give the pace to the entire pack. If it was the other way round, they would be left behind, losing contact with the pack. In case of an ambush they would be sacrificed. Then come five strong ones, the front line. In the centre are the rest of the pack members, then the five strongest following. Last is alone, the alpha. He controls everything from the rear. In that position he can see everything, decide the direction. He sees all of the pack. The pack moves according to the elders' pace and help each other, watch each other.'

The caption is inaccurate – that's not how wolves work, and if they do have an alpha animal it's down to that animal's status as the main breeder rather than any inherent leadership qualities – but the very fact that it's been written at all demonstrates the appeal of the 'leading from the back' concept. It can also be seen in the famous book *Watership Down*, about a posse of rabbits who flee their warren. Their chief rabbit Hazel is not the biggest, strongest, cleverest or the best fighter, but by standing back and letting those rabbits who are each of those use their abilities as best they can, he proves himself the ideal leader. And that, in the end, is what it's all about. A good leader is judged not by his own actions but by those of the people around him.

DANGER

Let me not pray to be sheltered from dangers, but to
be fearless in facing them. Let me not beg for the
stilling of my pain, but for the heart to conquer it.

Rabindranath Tagore

There's a cartoon called 'Victorian Risk Assessment'
featuring two nineteenth-century explorers in plus-
fours standing on the edge of a gorge looking out over
a rickety rope bridge. 'This should be perilous,' says the
first one. 'Excellent,' replies his friend.

It's a nod to how we perceive our ancestors as much
more daring and gung-ho than we are. There are few
things with which humans have such a complex relationship as danger. We seem to spend much of our lives
trying to avoid it – endless health and safety precautions, harnesses to keep toddlers from running off,

warning signs and barriers everywhere, labels on everything, public service announcements at airports and train stations saying the bleeding obvious – but by the same token we're drawn to danger like moths to a flame. In times past there was enough danger around that people didn't need to seek it out. Now that our lives are so comfortable, we like to put ourselves in deliberate jeopardy by BASE jumping, donning wingsuits, climbing mountains, racing cars and motorbikes, and a hundred other activities which give insurance companies whatever the corporate equivalent of a heart attack is, but which we still seek out for one main reason: they make us feel alive. Danger involves staring death in the face and living to fight another day, and that sparks a huge surge of adrenalin whoever you are. How you deal with that adrenalin, and how you face danger, is down not just to your personality but your training. That's what the army does: trains you to deal with danger in the right way rather than the wrong way.

Danger sparks fear, a subconscious chemical reaction in our body which actually stops us from getting into danger in the first place. Fear as a pre-emptive mechanism is really valuable: it's what stops you from walking up to a grizzly bear in the wild and stroking it. When you're scared your nervous system goes onto red alert.

Your eyes widen so you can see more, your mouth opens both to bring in more air and also in preparation to shout a warning or for help, your blood pumps faster and your breathing gets quicker.

When confronted with a dangerous situation, there are four possible reactions: fight, flight, freeze or fawn. The first two are adaptive and instinctual; the second two are more learned and reliant on social conditioning. Each of them can be good or bad depending on the nature of the situation.

FIGHT

This is a soldier's default mode, obviously. We don't train for years and make ourselves among the best fighters in the world if not to engage in combat when it actually occurs. That's what all the training's for, to bypass any natural propensity towards any of the other three reactions; and the fight reflex is also termed an approach-motivated reflex appealing to extraverts and risk-takers, who are often attracted to forces life.

The best way out of any dangerous situation is to make it less dangerous, and when in contact with the enemy nine times out of ten the best way to do that is to kill or injure as many of them as you can in order to neutralise their firepower and convince the ones who are left that their best course of action is to turn tail and live to fight another day. But there are times when fight isn't the best option, hard as that can be to accept for a bunch of highly skilled operators with their adrenalin up and their senses buzzing. For example, if you're vastly outnumbered but haven't yet been seen by the enemy, it may make more sense to stay hidden – in effect, to freeze, but deliberately so – and wait either till the enemy have moved on or until you have enough firepower to level up the playing field a bit. We would do this consistently on operations. It's the whole reason why Special Forces around the world prefer to operate during the darkness of night – so we can get into a location or target without being overwhelmed. Or if you're on a clandestine mission where the entire point is not to engage the enemy – for example, acting as forward spotters to direct air strikes – you would also try to minimise your fight reaction as much as possible, and blend into the local population so that no one would know what you are doing there.

FLIGHT

The temptation when faced with danger to turn and run as fast as possible in the opposite direction can be pretty overwhelming. Flight is an avoidant-motivated reflex which appeals to neurotic people among others. In the military it's rarely an option: you're almost always defending a position or trying to dominate an area so that the enemy can't get a foothold there, and turning tail in those circumstances just isn't going to happen. Every self-respecting soldier hates the idea of retreat, no matter how justified it might be. Flight equates with all the things soldiers hate: weakness, being inferior, even surrender.

But in the kind of situations you're more likely to come across in civilian life, flight can sometimes be the best option. Say you're walking home late one night, minding your own business, and you're suddenly surrounded by a group of blokes who aren't there to ask you for the time or to come and have a beer with you. They're drunk and egging each other on; they are most likely going to beat you up and nick your phone and wallet.

What are your options? You can fight them, but unless you're Jason Bourne you're not going to make much headway when you're so heavily outnumbered. You can freeze and hope the problem just magically goes away, but that's vanishingly unlikely. You can fawn in an attempt to make them take pity on you and leave you alone, but that's not how drunk blokes in a group work. So your best bet is, if you get even the smidgeon of a chance, to leg it. They might chase, but there's a good chance these kind of blokes are overweight, unfit and have no chance of outrunning you.

FREEZE

In some ways, freezing is the worst thing you can do. If you're in a dangerous situation and you freeze, you're not doing either of the things you need to do: either make the situation less dangerous or remove yourself from it if it remains dangerous. The problem is that freezing is a very natural reaction, and made more so by the kind of lives many of us lead, where we've eliminated so much danger that we can't even comprehend it when it does happen. You can see it in video footage of terrorist attacks, car crashes and other incidents: there are always some people who just stand there even when everyone else is fleeing, which itself should make the herd instinct kick in. Freezing is an extension of surprise. In essence, it can be the prelude to either fight or flight, the moment or two when you're processing a whole bunch of unfamiliar information in order to make the best decision. As we'll see later in the chapter, we deliberately use this tactic in the Special Forces, a brief time out in a stressful situation, but the difference is that we remain in control of the freeze rather than vice versa.

There are a few occasions when freezing is a good option, though. If you're hidden from a source of danger and you think that exposing yourself is going to be a worse option, then staying where you are is probably best. And in certain cases of encounters with wild animals, freezing is a good way of not presenting yourself as a threat to them and thereby dissuading them from attacking (but this by no means applies to all of them, far from it: with some it's better to back away slowly, with others it's recommended to make lots of noise and try to frighten them away).

The opposite of freeze is equally as dangerous. Some people when exposed to danger go into panic, otherwise known as 'flapping'. This is when panic takes over and the ability to make sound decisions is greatly affected. Believe me, I've seen this happen many a time. Some people can cover it well but inside they're flapping hard. This is also easy to spot if you've seen it play out, and it's not pretty. It has to be gripped before it exposes the team to danger through shit decisions.

FAWN

This is a little different from the other three, in that it is by a long way the most learned of reactions: less evolutionary and more conditioned, especially in those who've suffered abuse and whose immediate reaction when in danger is to try to defuse it. Fawning involves abasement, begging, crying and pleading with the source of danger not to harm you. The sad truth is that in most dangerous situations fawning will either make no difference whatsoever or it will actually make things worse: someone who poses a threat, armed and with their adrenalin up, is liable to become even more agitated by someone fawning rather than find themselves being calmed down. Perhaps the only situations in which fawning works are when the source of danger doesn't know that they're being threatening and doesn't intend to be, or as a tactic to make the threat discount you as someone to be reckoned with and therefore increase your chances of a surprise counter-attack (in which case this isn't really fawning at all but play-acting.)

So how do we deal with danger in a way which minimises it without compromising the mission? The mission here doesn't have to be a military one: it can be anything you intend to do which requires training, skill and bravery.

The documentary *Free Solo* is a good example. It charts the story of the free soloist Alex Honnold and his ascent of the 900-metre vertical rock face of El Capitan in California's Yosemite National Park. He was the first person ever to free solo the face, and for a good reason: it had long been thought impossible. Free soloing is exactly what it sounds like: climbing alone without ropes or any other safety equipment. If you fall from any height above a few metres, that's it: you're dead. It sounds insanely dangerous, and to most people – even many experienced climbers – it is.

But Honnold took several measures to minimise the risk and put himself in a place where the danger was not only manageable but also faced exclusively on his own terms. First, he trained incredibly hard, ensuring that his strength, fitness and flexibility were all top-notch. Second, he scouted the route many, many times beforehand, always with ropes and safety equipment. He took copious notes and made sure he knew exactly what moves he needed to perform on any given section. He didn't just do these moves once or twice: he did them until they were more or less muscle memory, second nature. Finally, he chose a day where weather conditions were perfect: dry and cool, so he would have no problems with rain slicking the rock and making grip hard, or with temperatures which were either freezing or scorching. All these meant that the danger was minimised because Honnold had eliminated so many of the personal, technical and meteorological variables which might otherwise have scuppered his climb. In fact, the danger arguably appeared greater than it was only because the consequences of any mistake would have been so severe. His chances of falling were very low, but if he had fallen he would inevitably have been killed.

Therefore training is a big part of facing danger, not just to reduce the risks but to get the body and mind used to the sensation of fear. The more you expose yourself to a situation which triggers fear, the less frightening it becomes. Repetition equals acclimatisation. Honnold, like anyone who operates successfully in dangerous conditions, had the holy trinity of dealing with danger locked down: exposure, knowledge and commitment. He'd *exposed* himself to the dangers of that particular climb not just day after day or week after week but month after month. He'd accumulated more *knowledge* about the climb than anyone else before him. And he was totally *committed* to executing the mission successfully. The fear which the danger produced wasn't a negative emotion at all: it kept him sharp and focused all the way to the top and a history-making climb.

One of the reasons *Free Solo* was so popular was that the risk of falling is one of the most common forms of danger, and the fear of it is one of the most powerful and primal fears there is. Part of SAS Selection is jumping into water from ten metres up. Ten metres is a long way up if you're not used to it, and a few people weren't; they couldn't do it. I was like, if you thought it was going to be a problem why haven't you gone and practised somewhere? Plenty of public pools have got ten-metre boards. There's no skill or technique involved in jumping off a board: it's purely and simply a case of mind over matter. And when the instructor says, 'Go' you go, just like you would on the battlefield.

Those who couldn't do the jump never came from the Paras, of course: jumping from heights is the Paras' essential purpose. I've done hundreds of parachute jumps in my time, and though they became almost routine the fear never totally left me, and nor should it have. Jumping out of a plane is no time for complacency, whether it's your first time or your thousandth. But for the most part daytime jumping is pretty easy. You rely so much on visuals as a parachutist, not just of the ground below you (how near you are to it and how closely you're sticking to your course) but of your fellow jumpers too. On a sunny day in the US, where The Regiment like to train, there are few better places to be than dropping out of the sky.

Night jumping is a different kettle of fish altogether. No one likes to jump at night, let alone into hostile areas. During the day you can see the rest of your team in the sky, so there's less chance of a collision. If someone flies into you, you're fucked. And being fucked at 25,000 feet in the air isn't pretty. There's a lot of room for error and when it goes wrong, it goes seriously wrong. The best thing that could happen to you is that you die on impact. And this is all before getting to the target and carrying out the mission.

Standing by the open door of a plane high above the earth's surface looking out into pitch blackness and thinking the same thought over and over again: what I'm about to do is fucking insane. Blotting that thought out with two other thoughts, deliberately more rational to steer myself away from the amygdala, the place in my brain where the fear responses reside. The first counter-thought is this: fuck's sake, this is what I joined to do, I'm in the fucking SAS. This is my responsibility, this is what I've trained for, this is what I do. The second is the same equation that Honnold faced: if I've prepared properly and if I actually break down a parachute jump into its constituent parts, then things are very unlikely to go wrong, but if things do go wrong then I'm in a whole world of shit. The first counter-thought is a kick up the arse; the second is arguably more helpful in terms of putting the fear in its place. It's not that I don't feel fear, but setting risk up like that it seems manageable and makes me more inclined to jump. As the RAF parachute training school motto has it: 'Knowledge dispels fear'. That, and the fact that there are half a dozen blokes behind me waiting for me to go, so refusing to jump isn't even an option. Then the dispatcher says, 'Stand by', and I know the next word is 'Go!', and on 'Go!' I jump come what may. In the military we're trained to work off words of command. The Russian physiologist Ivan Pavlov rang a bell and his dogs came running for dinner: our dispatcher says, 'Go' and I jump out into thin air. Same principle, and it goes for every aspect of military work: standing at a FUP (Forming-Up Point) about to conduct a live attack, waiting on the start line with a socking great log on my shoulder during Selection, anything and everything.

'Go!'

I jump out of the door. The wind snatches at me, the plane already swallowed up by the night. I think back to that first moment of freefall, the very first time I jumped from a plane. You never get that same feeling back. Even by the second time you're getting used to it, even though the fear never totally goes away. That first moment, standing on the edge of the unknown in every way: you can't quite recapture that, no matter how hard you try and how many times you jump.

If this is a combat situation rather than just an exercise, then the danger's hardly started. The funny thing about war is that even though it's incredibly dangerous, it's also baked into the human DNA. The ancient Greek philosopher Plato said that 'only the dead have seen the end of war', and it is as true now as it was then. There's a great quote in the Cormac McCarthy book *Blood Meridian* which sums it up perfectly. 'It makes no difference what men think of war, said the judge. War endures. As well ask men what they think of stone. War was always here. Before man was, war waited for him. The ultimate trade awaiting its ultimate practitioner.'

We're a belligerent species. We fight over anything and everything. We fight with our families, friends, colleagues and strangers. We're drawn to stories about conflict in whatever way that manifests itself; indeed, all drama is conflict one way or another, and without drama there's no story. We like reading about and watching dystopias, the more messed-up and brutal the better – there's no story in a utopia, no drama in perfection. And though many animals attack and kill each other, we're unique in that we do so because we choose to rather than as a survival imperative. When a fox goes into a chicken coop and kills every bird in there, it's not doing it to be nasty or to give itself a thrill. It does it because it's a carnivore and that's how it survives. Only humanity has a deliberate capacity for cruelty and its flipside, mercy. The fact that we continue to practise the first at least as much as the second is testament to the fact that though our societies have evolved far beyond those of animals, our brains haven't.

It is what it is and we are what we are. Any soldier who tells you there isn't a thrill to danger is lying. On my 2008 tour of Afghanistan, we used to sneak out at night to draw contacts from the Taliban. We'd try to flush them out and then get the mortar teams to bomb their positions. That sense of anticipation was intoxicating. We'd wait for first light and then they'd bite, and it'd all kick off. But we were so successful that after four or five consecutive nights of this they weren't so keen anymore. They'd talk on an open radio net with an unsecured signal which we could listen into, and our interpreter translated for us. 'Don't engage the guys with the green patches.' That's what they were saying. And I won't lie, we were all a bit disappointed when they wouldn't come out to play anymore. It was a much quieter tour than 2006 and we were desperate for some action, to put ourselves into danger and by doing so to feel that we were here for a reason rather than just marking time. But the harsh truth is that although it's all fun when everything is going right, when it goes wrong it hurts.

It was on that 2006 tour that Bryan Budd was killed, and the circumstances not just of that day but of the events leading up to it are good examples of how he dealt with danger. There were two incidents cited on his VC. The first took place on 27 July. It was the day we'd arrived back in Sangin after a few weeks rotated out to another part of Helmand, and the moment we got there we remembered what a shithole it was. Afghanistan wasn't exactly big on five-star resorts, but even by local standards Sangin was about as grim as it got. Bryan was sent out on patrol straight away: a marking of our territory, if you like, a display that we were here and we were going to boss things aggressively from now on.

The patrol walked through the town and the old bazaar, checking things out and making their presence felt. One of Bryan's men saw two Taliban gunmen on a rooftop. Suddenly rounds started flying from two or three directions at once, and Eddie Edwards, one of the privates, was hit twice, shattering his femur and opening his leg up from the thigh all the way down to the knee. Badly injured, he fell to the ground, still exposed to hostile fire and a sitting duck for any Taliban fighter who could get his aim right. Bryan knew that they wouldn't be able to get Eddie out without first eliminating the enemy threat, so he located the building from where the heaviest fire was coming and charged it. He could have been hit at any time, but this was what he needed to do – this was the only way to get Eddie out. So Bryan charged the building and sent the Taliban fighters packing, fleeing across an open field where they were engaged by some of the other lads. The casevac came in for Eddie, and the medics managed to save his leg.

The day Bryan died, 20 August, was another routine patrol close to Sangin district centre, the local government's administrative compound. It was five days before he was due to go home, but that's the thing about danger: it can strike anytime. Some blokes might have been half-switched off and thinking about home, but Bryan was such a professional that he would have been as on it as though it was the first day. We were doing a platoon clearance patrol to find a new path through the area north of the base, which meant blowing holes through a series of compound walls.

Bryan was leading an eight-man section on the right forward flank through a cornfield with stalks so high you couldn't see people over the top of them, like this was some Stephen King horror story out in the Midwest of America. He spotted some Taliban ahead – no more than 30 metres or so, but in that field 30 metres was a long way. Using hand signals, he ordered his men to flank left and move up undetected so as to keep the element of surprise, but the Taliban caught sight of another flank of the patrol and the advantage was gone.

Bryan didn't hesitate. Just as he had the previous month when Eddie had been hit, he went straight on the offensive. The Taliban began to lay down some serious fire, hitting three of Bryan's lads – one in the shoulder, one in the upper arm and face, and one in the chest plate of his body armour, hard enough to send him flying as though he'd been smacked by a baseball bat. That was three down out of eight, and still the fire kept coming. If they stayed where they were they could all have been wiped out. Bryan kept going, sacrificing himself to save the others' lives. It was insanely, ridiculously brave, to do that without any close support, and he must have known how much the odds were against him or anyone in that situation, but he kept going, kept attacking and killed several Taliban as he rushed their position.

I was part of the section sent to get him. I knew he'd probably be dead, but you always cling to whatever hope you can find in these situations. I cut through the cornfield and spotted him right away, his body surrounded by three of the Taliban he'd killed. There could have been more Taliban fighters just waiting for the recovery party, or booby traps around his body, but I didn't give a fuck. The sight of one of your blokes dead, let alone someone who'd been my own personal hero, outweighed everything else going on around me. I tried to give him CPR, but it was no good. I heard enemy fire in the distance, but it wasn't close enough for me to need to pay it much mind. I looked around me, saw that it was all safe and got on the comms to say I needed extraction.

Then I picked Bryan up, or at least tried to. Until you try to lift a dead body you have no idea how hard it is. It wasn't just his weight, though that was bad enough: he wasn't an especially big lad, but with all his kit and equipment he must have been 100 kilos easy, maybe more. It was that dead weight is just that: dead. It's awkward and it shifts around when and where you don't want it to, with limbs slopping down all over the place and forcing you to constantly adjust your own centre of gravity. Add to this the fact that I've got on 20 kilos or so of kit myself, and it's August in Afghanistan so it's hot as hell, and you can imagine how hard it was. If there had been any Taliban around I'd have been a sitting duck. Eventually a Scottish lad called McManus arrived. McManus was a big hard jock lad and he put Bryan on his back – not easily, not by a stretch, but at least more easily than I had. From there we made it back to the rendezvous point and were extracted back to base.

There was a real sense of shock in the base that night. You always know it might happen, and almost every platoon loses blokes in a war, but it's still different when it happens to you, and even more different when the bloke gone is someone who'd seemed so indestructible. Our CO, Lieutenant Colonel Stuart Tootal, said that 'Bryan died doing the job he loved, leading his men from the front, where he always was. He was proud to call himself a paratrooper and we were proud to stand beside him.' Only the very bravest men doing the very bravest things get awarded the Victoria Cross, the highest award for gallantry in the face of the enemy that can be awarded to British and Commonwealth forces. Bryan received his posthumously, not just for the incident in which he was killed but for the one the previous month too.

The citation in part reads: 'Corporal Budd's conspicuous gallantry during these two engagements saved the lives of many of his colleagues. He acted in the full knowledge that the rest of his men had either been struck down or had been forced to go to ground. His determination to press home a single-handed assault against a superior enemy force despite his wounds stands out as a premeditated act of inspirational leadership and supreme valour. In recognition of this, Corporal Budd is awarded the Victoria Cross.' He was only the 13th person to get one since the end of the Second World War, more than 60 years previously, and just the second since the end of the Falklands War in 1982 – and I can't think of a more deserving recipient. Everyone in the Paras likes to think of themselves as courageous, and with good reason, but sometimes you meet someone who's just that little bit extra. Bryan was one of those.

But even decisions as brave as the ones that Bryan made don't take place in a vacuum. On both of those occasions he didn't just go blindly charging in. He would have worked out the situation, and the odds, and most of all figured out what the best course of action was not so much for him personally but for the unit as a whole. That takes time, even if that time is a second or two. Time slows down in combat, because your brain is working several levels faster than usual. If you're ever involved in something like a car crash, you can see the same phenomenon. Those few seconds before impact (assuming it's the kind of crash you can see coming rather than one which blindsides you) seem to last an age, as you're processing so many things at once. Most of the time in life our brains are ticking along in relatively low gear, as we're in situations which are familiar and which we trust. Only when we go into unfamiliar environments do our brains operate on a different level, rousing the body and the senses too.*

Often the best way to deal with danger is to use that time to take a step back and try to assess things as accurately as possible. The French intelligence agency makes a point of watching for this during training and selection: blokes who just charge into a situation without performing a proper assessment first will be failed just as surely as those who hesitate too long. In the army we call it the 'condor moment': during a contact, after the initial action and reaction, the commander should always take a moment to step back (both figuratively and if possible physically) and see what his options are. This goes back to the way the brain behaves during moments of high stress. In the Special Forces we were taught that the brain can process no more than nine pieces of information at any one time. Any more than that, and overload and confusion can set in. In a contact situation it's very easy for those pieces of information to mount up very fast. Where are the enemy? Have they

* Hospital midwives sometimes see pregnant women who are about to give birth coming in only to find that their contractions slow down dramatically, sometimes to the point where they're sent home again. Why? Home is a familiar environment where the woman's body feels secure and relaxed, whereas hospitals are unfamiliar and so the body involuntarily tenses (or more accurately, the brain signals the body to tense).

got any more coming? Those fighters moving over there, are they pushing back or coming closer? Where are the rest of your men? How badly injured is the bloke you saw go down a few seconds ago? Do you need to get on the net to call for air support and/or a casevac? One escape route's been closed off: where are the others? What are the chances of making it to the extraction RV? What about IEDs? That's nine right there and you've barely started. And these aren't just abstract pieces of information you can consider at your leisure: these are all life and death decisions.

Once your brain starts to overload it's like a short-circuiting computer. It's not a case of your brain just throwing out every item above the magic number of nine and continuing to process those existing nine perfectly: the overload and confusion can shut down even the most basic decision-making processes, meaning that you're doing nothing right. Remember too that soldiers frequently aren't starting from an optimal base-line for good decision-making. You're in country for months, being shot at every day: exhausted, jumpy, sleep-deprived, mildly malnourished (army rations aren't Cordon Bleu), and very far from the well-rested relaxed people who could make easy decisions without sweat.

In computing they call this moment the 'breakpoint' – 'an intentional stopping or pausing place in a computer program put in for debugging purposes'. Think of the breakpoint as a personal debugging. The best way to ensure that it works is through breathing properly. In any stressful situation, it's easy to let your breathing get away from you: adrenalin, anxiety and fatigue make your breathing short, shallow and ragged. Breathing deeply into the diaphragm, inhaling through the nose and out through the mouth, is an excellent way of telling your brain and body to calm down, regain control and not make rash decisions. Lift your head up to ensure that you can get as much oxygen as possible into your lungs; this also helps you look around and take stock. These few seconds can make all the difference. I've used it plenty of times, not just in combat but in any stressful situation: out in rough seas on exercises, or finding that one of my oxygen cylinders on the ascent of Manaslu was dodgy and not providing me with the air I needed.

Panic gets checked early or not at all. If you let panic get away from you it's very hard to get it back; much easier, and better, to nip it in the bud.* Fear left unchecked produces panic, and panic left unchecked is exponential: it overcomes not only the person

---

* It works the other way too, of course. If you feel yourself too calm and need to rev yourself up, for example for a public speaking appearance, a few short, sharp, quick breaths will get the brain and body primed. Politicians and actors do this the whole time.

experiencing it but spreads to those around him, sending them into flat spins. If everyone's breathing right, no one's panicking. Think of the type of soldier who needs to be calmest of all, the sniper. Top snipers are very aware of their breathing, and will always be sure not just to have their respiration rate down as low as possible before taking a shot but will actually fire between breaths (and if possible between heartbeats too as the heartbeat will affect shooting at longer distances).

Sometimes, dealing with danger means avoiding it if possible: flight not fight. We've all been in situations when the hairs on the back of our necks go up and we feel in our bones that something's wrong. (This was the case just before Bryan was involved in the first firefight mentioned above, the day we'd come back to Sangin: as the patrol was heading back to base they noticed that the town had gone quiet. Very quiet. Too quiet. That only meant one thing: there was a Taliban attack coming and the non-combatant locals knew well enough to keep their heads down until it had all blown over.) On another occasion in Afghanistan a few of us were sent to take out an IED factory in Nad-e Ali. We walked for three hours to get there, and right from the start it was eerie: mist on the river, an unusual coolness in the air and everyone observing total silence. It may have been coincidence, but sometimes you get days when things feel just a bit off from the start. When we got to the factory we laid up for a while to observe it and see who came in and out, but it looked to be empty. That was a warning sign if ever there was one: the intel we'd been given said that this place was producing IEDs nineteen to the dozen. We used ladders to get over the walls and went in. Empty. Absolutely empty. And dead silent too. The hairs on the back of my neck were standing to attention as though this was the Trooping of the Colour, and I felt my sphincter go from 50p to 1p in a tenth of a second. Something wasn't right here. Something definitely wasn't right. It was dark inside, so I took out my torch and began to play the beam over the ground and around the walls, looking for disturbed earth. It was hard to tell what might be disturbed earth and what was just usual bumpy ground, but either way it still didn't feel right.

'Hands down this place is rigged,' I whispered.

A couple of the others weren't so sure. I was. There was nothing specific I could put my finger on, but it was gut instinct, and that's rarely failed me over the years. Besides, gut instinct is itself only a combination of lots of perfectly valid things – survival desire, fear responses, pattern recognition, applied knowledge, educated guesses. It's not moonshine or voodoo. There are very good social and biological reasons for gut instinct.

This was an IED factory. If we had intel that it was operating, then by the same token they could easily have had intel that we were coming. Where better to rig booby traps than a factory that made the damn things? Any intel we could get from here – materiel, documents, that kind of stuff – would be worthless if we were all blown to kingdom come.

'Let's just follow our tracks back and get the fuck out of here,' I continued.

Luckily, I could see that enough of the others felt the same way that I did: it was written all over their faces. So we did the sensible thing and left, very slowly, very cautiously, very quietly and very alive.

The problem in situations like that, of course, is that it goes against the grain of all your training, not to mention your self-esteem and self-image, to do something which could be construed as cowardly. Rationally, it wasn't a cowardly thing to do at all: it was sensible. It wasn't refusing to come to a mate's help when he was pinned down or badly wounded. It was the best course for the most number of people. If one of us had triggered an IED, who knows? The whole place could have been rigged … that would have been one long night. When you've been in quite a few situations, you realise that the only person who can really judge what you're prepared to do is you yourself. I've been in scraps where we've called for back-up from QRFs (Quick Reaction Forces) or helicopter crews, and that back-up hasn't come. The blokes in charge of those forces or crews took the decision that it was too dangerous for them to come, that they only risked losing lives and equipment without much chance of actually rescuing us, and that the best course of action was to leave us to fight our way out of whatever trouble we were in and get to a prearranged and safe extraction point. It's easy in the heat of battle to curse them out for being weak and chickenshit, but that's when adrenalin's running high and you say a lot of things you don't necessarily mean. By the time you're back, and rested, and in the debrief, things take on a different hue. They explain why they took the decisions they did, and when they do it makes sense. I never judged a pilot for not wanting to go out or a QRF commander for wanting to stay in base. I couldn't see what they could at the time, I wasn't privy to the information they had. They have lots of considerations to take into account, their own men and equipment to protect, and if it was as easy as always rushing to the aid of everyone who asks for it then leadership wouldn't be as hard as it is.

Over the years, untold men have been killed because they were too scared to admit that they were scared. It takes a very brave man not just to admit his fear but actually to refuse to do something because of it.

Apart from that incident in the IED factory, I've had my fair share of dangerous situations in the mountains. When we were training in Chamonix for the aborted ascent of K2, we'd be out every morning before dawn so we could summit by mid-morning and be back before the sun had a chance to melt the snow and make conditions tricky. The last place you want conditions to be tricky is on a descent, not just because you're going in the same direction as gravity but also because it's human nature to switch off mentally, even slightly, when you're on the way home – and in the mountains – 'even slightly' can be terminal. So much of mountaineering is about reaching the summit, and it's easy to forget that the summit is only, at best, halfway. You still have to get down. On K2, something like a quarter of those who summit die on the way down. You're tired, you're exultant at having made it: these are the dangerous times, when your mind drifts to home and it's hard to keep your concentration exactly on point.

On Manaslu, which I discuss more fully in 'Excellence', there was a moment where I had to make a decision about how to deal with danger. We were near the summit, and for various reasons I wasn't in the best shape, but even if I had been I'd still have been cautious. There'd been a heavy fall of fresh snow, and the slopes were more than 35 degrees steep, a combination which my mountain course had taught me was prime condition for avalanches. There were a few small snow slides when we were up there – not big ones nor proper uncontrollable ones, but it still felt to me as though this was the mountain warning us. It was like the IED factory in Nad-e Ali: this doesn't feel right. If you get caught in an avalanche you're in a whole world of pain, as several things can mess you up: the simple weight and force of the snow, the lack of air if you're buried beneath one (more people die of suffocation in avalanches than impact), or even the wind which is caused by the falling snow pushing the air out of the way ahead of itself. I knew that no one wanted to be the first to turn around, but the moment I said I was heading back down almost everybody came with me (and the few who didn't never managed to summit anyway, as conditions had become too bad; mercifully, however, they weren't caught in an avalanche). It was one of the best decisions I ever made: I felt it was right from the moment I took it.

When it came to danger on the mountain, however, nothing beat Everest in 2019.

My first summit in 2017 had been such plain sailing as to have been almost blissful. This would be completely different. It was as though the mountain gods had said, 'Well, old son, we gave you an easy ride last time, so let's see what you're made of this time around.' For a start, there was a much smaller weather window for summiting than normal, which meant that many more climbers were making their ascents in a much shorter time period (hence that viral picture of the queue on top of the world), which in turn upped the risk considerably. Mountains are dangerous, and inexperienced climbers on mountains can also be dangerous.

I was guiding a group of seven climbers, and their experience levels were mixed. Some were extremely robust and strong; others needed more guidance. We all managed the acclimatisation phase OK. I took a few of the climbers up to Camp 3 before returning to rest at Base Camp: this is a standard process for the acclimatisation rotation window, to get your body adapted to the extreme altitude. But with the weather window so short we knew we'd have to rush, which in turn meant that we risked both pushing people too hard and not having the right supplies further up the mountain.

Still, we calculated the pros and cons, and decided that the odds were still in our favour. I left Base Camp with the group quite late on in the day, meaning that we wouldn't get a chance to rest at Camp 2 for long. We were climbing via the south side through the notorious Khumbu Icefall, with ice blocks double the size of your house slowly moving down the glacier. This is one of the most dangerous parts of the climb, as the crevasses we crossed on fixed ladders roped together were incredibly deep.

It was on our fast ascent to Camp 2 that one of my team, Geth, started to cough up blood. I had to make three decisions on the spot, all of them interlinked: what to do with Geth, what to do with the rest of the group and what I personally should do. I reckoned that there was enough experience in the group for them to carry on up to Camp 2 alone, allowing me to help Geth get to the safety of one of the spare tents at Camp 1. We managed to get into the tent at around 8 pm. We found a spare sleeping bag and I helped Geth get inside, allowing him to regulate his breathing and lessen further blood build-up in his lungs. We huddled tightly because by now it was about 20 degrees below zero. I radioed for one of our Sherpas to come down from Camp 2 with food and water-boiling kit. It must have been around midnight when the Sherpa arrived – he'd had a tough descent as there'd been a fresh snowfall – and by this time I'd started to shiver uncontrollably. I didn't have a sleeping bag in the tent (mine was back up at Camp 2) and although at this stage I was still feeling quite strong, I also knew I needed to move to generate heat to avoid hypothermia.

Danger can mutate: you nix one threat and find that another's sprung up in its place. I'd helped my teammate, but now I was in trouble.

So shortly after midnight, knowing that Geth was safe with the Sherpa, I set out on the nightmare climb back up to Camp 2, the one with which I began this book: a thin cone of light from my head torch cutting through the darkness; the only sounds the wild howl of the wind, the clinking of my carabiners and the ragged gasping of my own breath; so cold that I stopped shivering and began to go hypothermic; and most of all the vision of my own death.

When I finally got back to Camp 2, I was too exhausted to eat much; I just climbed into my sleeping bag and slept. Not surprisingly, there was a serious knock-on effect the next day. We went up to Camp 3, and it wasn't long into the climb that I thought, 'Hang on, I'm not feeling too good here.' I was running on empty and had gone to the well too often the day before. I felt a sudden build-up of diarrhoea inside me and only just managed to get my summit suit down in time. It was partly my body rebelling against yesterday's effort, and partly perhaps a psychosomatic reaction to the mental and emotional effort I'd spent on that climb. For an hour or so I couldn't move: I just had to let all this stuff come out of me. The others weren't looking too flash either – though they certainly looked better than me! – and we made the tough decision to turn around and head all the way back down to Base Camp. Again, we worked out the odds and decided to be sensible. The high reaches of Everest aren't the place to be fucking around.

As it turned out, that was a good call. No one from other parties who tried to summit the next day managed to make it, as the rope-fixing team weren't properly set up higher on the mountain. We spent a few good days down at Base Camp breathing the thicker oxygen and eating and sleeping well. By the time we pushed for our summit attempt again, we felt fit, well rested and eager to go. And when I made it this time, summiting the mountain with two other guys and Geth, after all the trauma, hardship and danger I shed a tear or two. I hadn't the first time up, but I did this time.

I knew I'd got lucky. That night climb from Camp 1 to Camp 2 could easily have ended in disaster. Sometimes you need a bit of luck. In my first Afghan tour, the only reason I wasn't killed during one contact when the Taliban opened up on us unexpectedly was that they most likely hadn't zeroed their weapons or they couldn't shoot in the first place. We were crossing an open area in Sangin while handling some detainees when suddenly all hell broke loose: rounds kicking up dust by our feet, all that kind of stuff. If they'd shot properly they'd have killed me before I had a chance to react. We called in the mortars, and that involved a whole lot of trust in our boys to get it right. A mortar's danger range is about 100 metres and its lethal range about 20, which wasn't much further than we were from the Taliban, so in calling in the round we were going to get blitzed ourselves if the mortars were even a fraction off. Luckily 3 Para's mortar teams were the best in the business, and they dropped the shells right where we needed them to. Even then, it was so close that when we got back to base and I was chatting to the mortar fire controller, he said he'd been so scared of fucking it up and killing us all that he'd felt a little bit of piss dripping down his leg.

I had an even luckier escape earlier that same tour. We were bunked up in the Governor's House in Sangin, and outside the house was this little garden space the Afghans who worked with us were really proud of. There was a washing line set up there, and I was just hanging out some of my clothes – yeah that's right, I can wash – when suddenly this mortar slammed into the wall nearby. Up till then all the firefights had just been bullets – this was the first time we'd been mortared, and for a team to be that accurate first up was phenomenal. I was knocked off my feet, flat onto my arse, head stunned and ears ringing. Through the smoke and dust

I saw everyone pegging it inside, so I pushed myself upright, checked that I had all the limbs I needed and no more than the usual amount of holes, and I ran inside like everybody else. We hauled arse down to the basement to wait it out, listening for the mortars being fired and then for their landing, as that way we could gauge distance and direction. When they'd finished we gave it another half hour just to be sure and then came out blinking into the sunlight. A shell had landed on the exact spot where I'd been hanging the washing out! I'd have been vaporised, absolutely vaporised. No decade in The Regiment, no Everest, no undercover ops – just 'Here lies what's left of Jay Morton, blown to smithereens while hanging out his grundies'. As a way to go, it wouldn't have been especially heroic.

The washing was ripped to shreds, of course. I've still got a piece of it somewhere: a good and necessary reminder that no matter how bad any given day has been, it could have been much, much worse. And I've still got a few of my nine lives left.

INTELLIGENCE

The measure of intelligence is the ability to change.

Albert Einstein

The word 'intelligence' has two meanings in the military. The first is what the majority of civilians understand by the word: the ability not just to acquire knowledge and skills but also to apply these to daily life. The second is information, particularly secret or classified information: uncovering it, gathering it, disseminating it, analysing it and acting on it. The first is never abbreviated to 'intel'; the second often is.

Both types of intelligence are important, but in different ways; and both types of intelligence come in several different forms.

INTELLIGENCE 1: KNOWLEDGE

Everyone knows what an IQ test is. It measures memory, analytical thinking and mathematical ability, and you can find any number of tests on the internet in ten seconds flat. Your score is still seen in many quarters as a shorthand for your intelligence: below a certain level you look actively stupid, above a certain level you get classified as a genius. There's even a club, Mensa, for those who score exceptionally highly. But IQ – intelligence quotient – is only one way to measure intelligence. There are at least two other ways, EQ (emotional quotient, which lets you make connections with other people) and AQ (adaptability quotient, which lets you deal with and exploit changing situations), and as a soldier I needed all three. I needed IQ to understand the situations I was presented with, EQ to forge bonds with my comrades and AQ to mentally shapeshift in fast-moving situations such as contacts. I couldn't have done my job without all of them. They're not entirely separate from each other: to an extent they're interdependent and interlinked, as they all help you solve problems, and in essence solving problems is what life, work and certainly soldiering is about.

Someone who has IQ and EQ but not AQ will be good at solving existing problems and dealing with the people they know, but will come unstuck when situations change and they have to deal with new ways of working. Someone who has IQ and AQ but not EQ will be able to solve problems not just now but also in the future; however, they won't be much good at working alongside people in either scenario. Someone who has EQ and AQ but not IQ will be a popular colleague and the first to put up their hand to volunteer for anything new, but whether they'll actually be any good at dealing with complex issues is another matter entirely.

First, IQ. Some kids excel right from the word go and are always top of the class in school. I was never one of them. I didn't enjoy school, I didn't do well academically – I was never the lad who got any prizes when it came to grades. It was as much an attention thing as anything else: if I wasn't interested in something then I wouldn't put any energy or effort into it. (Some things never change.) And I wasn't interested in school, because the way the lessons were conducted was so rigid and the subjects we were told to study were so boring. We were told that education was the only way forward and that education is everything. Your grades would determine which college you went to, your degree would determine which job you got, and your job would determine how much money you earned, how big your house would be, how flash your car, how expensive your holidays, and so on. It seemed to me then, and still seems to me today, to be a load of shit, all of it. Why make kids learn about Tudors and Stuarts if all you think they're good for is stacking shelves in supermarkets? School to me wasn't a well-planned system for producing rounded, ambitious and happy children: it was a gigantic childcare experiment, where parents went to work while teachers barely kept control of kids and taught them stuff by rote for no better reason than that was the way it had always been done.

I wasn't stupid, though you could be forgiven for thinking that I was, because schools measured intelligence only one way and that way didn't suit me or the way I approached life. Now, in my thirties, I can't get enough of some of those subjects that used to bore me to tears. I love history, geography and science. I read *Sapiens: A Brief History of Humankind* by Yuval Noah Harari, and it blew my mind. If history had been taught at my school the way Harari writes it then I'd have paid more attention. I've got a thirst for knowledge, not just to acquire it but to discuss it and apply it too. Maybe it's just because I'm older and more open to that kind of stuff these days, but at heart I'm still the same person

I was when I was a kid – I've still got the same personality traits as I did back then.

This is also why it annoys me when I hear parents talking to their kids in stupid voices, patronising or babyish. Kids are human beings just the same as adults are. Talk to them like human beings. They're people in and of themselves, and they're going to do what they're going to do. The best way to educate them is to be there for them, guide them, and try to stop them doing too much stupid shit while realising that they're always going to do some of that stupid shit anyway and that within reason it's good for them. Shoving kids in classrooms and boring them rigid is not a good way to educate them. To me it's amazing that in all these years we haven't come up with anything better.

If you'd asked my teachers whether I'd end up in the army they'd probably have said yes, that was always a possibility. If you'd asked them whether I'd end up in the Special Forces, where only thinking soldiers make it and where intelligence and independence of thought are not just valued but essential, they'd have been more doubtful, and that's a polite way of putting it. But I couldn't have made it into the SAS without being intelligent. Any image of Special Forces soldiers as just thick lunks who think they're Rambo is totally wrong. In the Green Army, you're doing general soldiering with general aims. As a Para in Afghanistan, for example, I was there to try to make an area safe and deny the Taliban as much time, space and opportunity as possible. Pretty much everything we did was within the parameters of what we'd been trained for. It was exciting and challenging, sure, but it didn't need too much brainpower. But in the SAS I carried out specific missions with surgical purposes: detain this individual, take out this factory, uncover this piece of intel. The variety was much greater, and therefore so too was the need for lateral thinking and intelligence. In the SAS you have to think your way round and through problems rather than just blast your way through them (though sometimes all the thinking leads you to the conclusion that blasting your way through is in fact the best strategy, in which case happy days).

Lateral thinking for me has always been a key part of intelligence: approaching a problem from an angle no one else has considered. There's a story about the American rock band Van Halen which illustrates this perfectly. Back in the 1980s they used to have a clause in their rider (the list of food, drink and other items the band gets supplied with at a venue) which stipulated that they were to be given bowls of multi-coloured M&M sweets with all the brown ones taken out. If they found a single brown M&M, the band would be entitled to cancel the show and still get paid the full whack, so the promoter rather than them would take the financial hit. At the time, this was seen as just another example of rock stars being dicks because they could be: why on earth would you want all the brown M&Ms taken out, and on pain of a hugely expensive forfeiture, except to show how spoilt and entitled you were?

As it turned out, there was a very good reason for the stipulation (which the band called Clause 126). Putting on a rock concert involves a whole load of complex equipment and systems, any of which could go wrong with serious consequences unless they were properly installed and checked. Van Halen's contracts were hundreds of pages long, and the band didn't have the time to go through every point line by line when they got to a new stadium or arena to check that the venue's management had done everything they'd agreed. So the brown M&Ms clause was their shortcut, a canary in the mine: a quick and pretty foolproof way of seeing whether the venue's management had read every line of the contract and implemented all the necessary measures. If they hadn't read the contract properly, who knows what else they'd missed? So every time Van Halen found brown M&Ms backstage they'd call a complete line check, inspecting every aspect of the sound, lighting and stage set-up to make sure it was perfect. Nine times out of ten they'd find problems.

We didn't use M&Ms in the SAS, but we used the same principle: find creative ways to solve problems which might otherwise seem insurmountable. And, as I said in the 'Leadership' chapter, these ways can come from anyone in the unit, not just the most senior people. In the Green Army you do what you're told and don't argue, unless you want to find yourself up on charges of insubordination or worse. You follow the instructions of the bloke senior to you and you don't think much about the bigger picture. You might be a genius or you might be an idiot; it doesn't matter either way, because what you think is largely irrelevant. Follow orders, do your job and you'll be grand. But Special Forces soldiers use brains first and balls second: we think for ourselves and take the initiative rather than blindly following orders from above. You could be deployed to an area where you have no one in charge of you or no formal leadership. You have to use your initiative to figure out what it is that you must do there. And to do that you need intelligence.

Often in the SAS you're given a piece of kit and told that you've got an hour or so to learn how to use it: not just how to use it in general terms but how to use every last little bit of it, every feature and capability it has, and to be able to use those features and capabilities in the dark, by touch alone, as if you've been doing it for years. You have to learn how to use things as though your life depends on it, as often it will. Knowing how to distil all that knowledge quickly and effectively is intelligence. The astronaut Chris Hadfield showed it when he took the manual for the International Space Station – which, as you can imagine, is vast (the manual not the ISS, though the ISS is too), and boiled all the important points down into a few note cards. Barristers have to do this all the time: wade through hundreds, sometimes thousands of pages of documents, and pull out the important points which they can then use in court. And of course those important points don't come with 'IMPORTANT POINT' typed in thick red ink all over them. The crucial piece of evidence which sways the case could be something tiny hidden in a dense passage of text, something which could easily be missed. Speed reading while being alert for key information is a big ask, but it's also an important one.

On SAS ops those small details were just as important, and you needed intelligence to spot and apply them. Suicide bombers were a case in point. When I was first in Afghanistan with 3 Para we were given very basic instructions about how to identify potential suicide bombers: they'd have shaved their heads, they'd be talking to themselves, they'd be sweating and agitated, all that kind of stuff. But of course suicide bombers aren't always so obliging as to walk around looking like the kind of nutter who'd arouse suspicion in a moron. So we had to use our brains and look beyond the obvious: trying to spot micro-behaviour, little ticks which were just a bit off, even someone behaving too casually rather than too obviously weirdly. As with the IED factory in Nad-e Ali, it was partly instinct, but again that instinct is based on many factors.

There's a very good and effective commercial in the US which shows what I mean about looking beyond the obvious. It features a teenage boy called Evan who's under-motivated at school and longing for the summer holidays, something I could definitely relate to. 'I am bored,' he carves into a library table. The next day, he finds that someone's written 'Hi Bored, nice to meet you' in reply. (This never happened to me at school, sadly.) He and his unknown pen pal write more and more to each other, and as Evan goes about his school day he's always looking to see who she might be: someone in his class, or the cafeteria, or in the hallways. Finally, on the very last day of term, he meets her in the school gym, and as they smile and chat the gym doors open behind them … and another pupil drops his bag, pulls out a semi-automatic and opens fire.

'While you were watching Evan,' a caption says, 'another student was showing signs of planning a shooting. But no one noticed.' Then the commercial rewinds and we see some of the same scenes again, this time with our eyes on the shooter kid who we missed first time round as he was always in the background. We see him reading a guns and ammo magazine, being bullied by other students, making a finger pistol behind a teacher's back, sitting on his own in the cafeteria while everyone else is in groups, and watching a shooting video on the library computer. All easy signs to miss, even for intelligent people, unless that intelligence is used wisely.

In the army we were taught the seven questions which need to be asked and answered before combat.

- What are the enemy doing and why?
- What have I been told to do and why?
- What actions/effects do I want to have on the enemy?
- Where can I best accomplish each action/effect?
- What resources do I need to accomplish each action/effect?
- When and where do these actions take place in relation to each other?
- What control measures do I need to impose?

These questions between them not only cover all necessary bases; they also enforce consistent and rigorous critical and analytical thinking. As such, they are easily transferable to civilian life. In fact, I used them when working with ThruDark in the early stages.

- *What are the enemy doing and why?* For 'enemy' here, we substituted 'the market' and/or 'competitors'. The outdoor clothing market is a very competitive one, and contains both big established players such as North Face and smaller, more niche ones. Each of these companies has their own approach to market in terms of product range, price points and customer profile. Only by knowing and understanding these approaches could we see how best to position ourselves, both to tap parts of the market previously dormant and also take business from our competitors.
- *What have I been told to do and why?* This was both a personal and a collective question. On one level, it was one for me to answer individually: what was my role within the company as distinct from Staz and Louis's? What was my job description, what were my responsibilities, what were my obligations? I had to ensure both that I was happy with the extent of my job and also that it dovetailed with their

responsibilities and expectations. Between us we needed to have all the basics of running a company covered. It's like arcs of fire in the military: you want to have a bit of overlap between you to provide back-up and failsafe options, but not so much that areas are left uncovered. Two people doing exactly the same thing leaves room for no one doing something else which might be necessary. As in the army, we looked for both specified and implied activities – the first being written down and contracted, the second widely understood but perhaps unspoken. The 'why' part of the question was about aims: what were our objectives and how would we define success? Success is both tangible (turnover, profit, market share, investment levels) and intangible (job satisfaction, rewarding working environment). To some extent we went from right to left first and then left to right; i.e. by starting at the end (objectives in the foreseeable future) we could build back through interim objectives to the present day, analysing as we went, and only then did we reverse the flow and build up the actions needed from now through to completion.

- *What actions/effects do I want to have on the enemy?* Again, for 'enemy' read 'market'. The actions we wanted were to gain a route to market, which we could accomplish in three ways: direct selling online, through retailers, or a combination of both. Each approach has pros and cons in terms of pricing and consumer visibility, so we needed to work out what our best option was. The effects we wanted were, of course, first and foremost to be a viable business – so many businesses go bust in the first year or two – but beyond that to establish ourselves as the go-to supplier of choice for those who really valued and/or needed the best products on the market.

- *Where can I best accomplish each action/effect?* This involved various things: creating a detailed outline plan; developing a breakdown structure which divided the project into smaller, more easily deliverable components; working out and securing all the necessary resources; and drawing up a schedule to factor in cash-flow and effective action sequencing. In the army we use the term 'intent' – basically, the effects you intend to achieve come what may, so that while circumstances may change, the brief will not. We took all these steps with the intent in mind.

- *What resources do I need to accomplish each action/ effect?* As an outdoor clothing company there are several interlinked parts to our business, all of which we classify as resources. We need a factory to make the clothes, and we searched long and hard before finding the right one. We need distribution networks to get the clothes from the factory to us and then from us to the customers. We need marketing in several forms: our own website, social media, appearances in press and on TV. We need regulatory compliance basics such as bookkeeping, accountancy, company filings and so on.

- *When and where do these actions take place in relation to each other?* This is partly about ensuring that all systems are operating optimally and that the left hand knows what the right hand is doing. If a magazine wants to do a shoot with our kit, for example, we have to be able to get them the right kit on time, or they won't run the piece and we'll have lost a marketing opportunity. But this also gives an opportunity to stress test the various working practices we have and see how they'd fare when the shit hits the fan, because along with death and taxes one of life's inevitabilities is that sooner or later there will be a massive shit/fan interface. The army is big on contingency plans, and we factored these in to our thinking: how would we cope if the factory went bust, for example, or one of our core team members became critically ill?

- *What control measures do I need to impose?* It's no good just putting a plan in place and thinking that it's done for good. We needed to find ways of monitoring progress in all areas on a regular basis, as only by doing so could we check that we were continuing to go in the right direction. For example, it's not enough just to have regular meetings with each other: we needed to know what these meetings needed to cover, what data we needed to hand, what issues we needed to discuss ahead of time, and so on.

I've used ThruDark as an example, but these seven questions are applicable across the board. They help you make decisions based on intelligence and rational analysis rather than emotion, semi-formed hunches (hunches are for TV detectives or Richard III only) or one of my biggest bugbears, the sunk costs fallacy. It's very easy to want to continue with a course of action because you've committed time, effort and money to it. This course can be anything: a career path, a house move, a relationship. This is the sunk cost fallacy – that because you've spent so much on something you must keep it going as otherwise it'll all have been for nothing. It's a very easy way of thinking to fall into, and a very understandable one too, but it's also entirely wrong.

The intelligent thing to do with any course of action is to assess it as critically, thoroughly and dispassionately as possible. Sunk costs, the ones already committed to the project, have gone: they're in the past and can't be changed. Present costs and prospective (future) costs are what's important here.

An army has been in a foreign country for many years at a cost of billions and still hasn't achieved its objectives. Should that army stay there or be withdrawn? The billions spent are the one thing which decision-makers should ignore: they've gone and have no bearing on the current situation. Does the army stand any chance of achieving its objectives? Can those objectives be changed in the light of new circumstances? Is there still the political will and public support back home for continued involvement? Can the current and future costs be justified? These are the considerations which the decision-makers will need to include.

You've been in a relationship for five years. Should you end it or get married? Again, the one thing which is irrelevant here is the five years. If you start thinking of all the sunk costs – 'Well, if we split up then those years have been a total waste, and I could have met someone else in that time' – then you may be tempted to hang on to a relationship which isn't right because you've already invested so much together. The questions you need to ask are: Do I see a future with this person? Are our interests and values sufficiently aligned for me to want to make a life with them? Do I think we can weather the inevitable storms? If we want to have kids, do we have similar views on how to raise them? This will help you see more clearly and make the right decision, even if that's an incredibly painful one in the short term.

You've been doing the same job for a decade. Should you continue or switch careers? Again, the sunk costs – the years, the effort, perhaps the training and qualifications you've busted your nuts to get – aren't the issue here. As discussed in 'opportunities', I had this myself when leaving the SAS. I'd been there ten years and was well regarded, so I had a more or less guaranteed continued career progression if I wanted it. But I didn't, and most crucially I didn't think of those ten years as a waste. I thought of them as having taught me a hell of a lot, having been huge fun and provided me with not only brilliant experiences but also mates for life, and having given me skills which were easily transferable into other areas. And I think these factors are really important no matter the situation, as they're more or less the opposite of sunk costs: they're the visible benefits of something which may no longer be right but which had a lot of upsides at the time. A relationship which goes sour will still have had its good times and will have taught you a lot about yourself, about other people and about relationships themselves. An army in country can still have improved the lives of lots of people there even if the overall mission didn't turn out to be successful. It's too easy to label something either a total success or a total failure, whereas the reality is that most things are in between.

Assessing which is which is arguably as much a question of EQ as IQ; that is, being open to factors which are more about feeling than thinking, which defy easily quantifiable metrics. EQ is just as important as IQ in everyday life, and in some ways more so: we all know someone who might be intellectually very bright indeed but who has little idea of how to deal with the world as it is, is socially inept and awkward, and is therefore unhappy and/or unsuccessful. EQ enables you to get along with colleagues and friends, which is in turn vital to creating an environment where teamwork is encouraged, lauded and rewarded.

Many of the competitors at the Invictus Games for wounded, injured or sick service personnel spoke warmly of Prince Harry's emotional intelligence, not just in founding the Games themselves because he realised the need for them (to give the competitors something to work towards, to let them experience the camaraderie and piss-taking of a quasi-military environment again, to use sport as part of a healing and rehabilitation process), but also in the way he was with the competitors themselves, instinctively seeing himself as one of them (a soldier) rather than a man apart (a prince). If you have little interest in other people or few solid ways of relating to them, then you won't be much of a team player, and most environments in life require you to be one to a greater or lesser extent.

EQ is divided into four main categories: self-awareness, self-management, empathy and relationship-building.

- *Self-awareness.* Knowing your strengths,
  weaknesses and trigger points is invaluable.
  Everyone has emotions, and often these emotions –
  particularly negative ones – can be seen as
  inconvenient, shameful or unhelpful. It's easy to be
  self-aware when you're feeling great, happy and
  motivated, but less easy if for whatever reason
  you're feeling shame, anger, envy, weakness or
  resentment. The temptation is to put those away in
  a box and suppress them rather than deal with
  them. Soldiers are no better at dealing with negative
  emotions than anyone else, and indeed in some
  ways are worse at it: we're not especially

encouraged to share our feelings, even though things on that front are better than they were in terms of counselling offered and so on. 'Crack on' was the unofficial army motto. Cracking on is the right course if you're aware enough to deal with the bad stuff, but if you're not then it just risks sweeping the problems under the carpet and having them bite you in the arse later down the line.

- *Self-management.* You might have little control over when you experience emotions, but you *do* have control over how you deal with them. You can talk to someone you trust, or work out anger through physical exercise, or find solace in nature by long forest walks, or any other number of techniques. It doesn't matter what you choose as long as it helps you process the emotions. There's a fine balance to be had between pushing negative emotions away and letting them take you over entirely, and this balance is dealing with them in a healthy way. The person who does this is also likely to be adept at other aspects of self-management, such as self-control, trustworthiness and conscientiousness. People who self-manage well also tend to look after themselves physically by taking exercise, eating well and resting the right amount, which has benefits across the board: as the ancient Romans said, *mens sana in corpore sano* (a healthy mind in a healthy body). Uncontrolled stress, which is usually negative emotions in one form or another, raises blood pressure, suppresses the immune system, increases the risk of heart attacks and strokes, contributes to infertility and speeds up the aging process. And in the short term, as we saw in 'danger', poor self-management in high-stress situations can lead to poor decision-making, which can in turn have serious consequences.

- *Empathy.* It's easy to become so wrapped up in our own problems, issues and lives that we don't give enough thought to other people. Empathy is about more than just being interested in those around us, however. It's being open not just to what they're doing but also to how they're feeling; not just what they're saying but also what they're not saying. If you ask your mate how they are and they say, 'Fine.' it may be that they are indeed fine; or it may be that something's bothering them and they're covering that up. An empathetic person will notice that and ask if they can be of any help. They may get rebuffed – 'Mate, I said it's nothing, just leave it' – but at least they will have let the other person know they care, and that person may want to talk more at a later date. One of the best pieces of advice I heard about how to deal with someone who's upset about something is to approach it in a twofold way. First ask, 'Would you like to talk about it or not?', and if they say yes then ask the follow-up question, 'Are you looking for me to help find a solution, or do you just want someone to listen to you?' Men in particular are very prone to try to fix things, including whatever's gone wrong in the lives of those close to them, but sometimes the best course is just to let someone unload. Empathy also works on a group as well as an individual level – the ability to 'read a room' and see what the collective dynamics are and how to deal with them.

- *Relationship building.* You will rarely go wrong with good interpersonal skills. Relationship building is not just about being able to connect with your mates or colleagues. It's about using influence and being able to persuade people, about communicating clearly and honestly, about being able to manage conflicts and resolve disagreements in healthy and constructive ways, about working towards common goals and creating group synergy as part of this, and of course about leadership too. Humour is a vital part of these, and many people with a good sense of humour also have high EQ (there are some who don't, but their humour tends to be cold, nasty and at other people's expense). EQ also involves realising that disagreements are inevitable in group situations, and are not in fact things to be scared of - quite the opposite. Disagreements allow issues to be aired and people to feel heard, which in turn allow them to grow closer to others.

I needed all four of these during my army career, and in spades. And I didn't use them just in terms of relations with and towards my fellow soldiers either. I used them with the local populations of those countries where we were deployed. British troops in the Iraqi city of Basra liked to patrol in berets rather than helmets whenever possible: it made us look less threatening and more approachable. In Afghanistan we often came across small kids, and again whenever possible I'd go down on one knee to be nearer their height and try to let them know I meant them no harm, offering them sweets or chocolate. On one occasion when I was doing this I felt a nudge from behind, and it was an old bloke in a dish-dash offering me an ice-cream, so I figured I must be doing something right. Getting the local population onside was really important: I reckon only about 5 per cent were Tier One Taliban (active fighters), and even factoring in what we called Tier Two (those who'd support the Taliban by offering shelter, storing weapons, running messages, etc.), that still left the vast majority of the population who weren't trying to kick us out or kill us, and they were the ones we needed to convince of our bona fides. Armies talk about winning the hearts and minds of the local populations, but you can't do this without genuine EQ.

Of course, even on the most benign and uneventful patrols things can change very fast indeed, which is where the third of the Qs, AQ, came in. One of the most important aspects of soldiering was thinking on your feet, constantly reacting and adapting to changes. A small change could presage a big change – such as Sangin going quiet before the first attack on Bryan Budd's patrol – and so you couldn't afford just to wait for the big changes and ignore the little ones. Being a soldier is rather like paddleboarding: no matter how calm and serene it appears, you're always metaphorically shifting your weight, reacting to constant little adjustments around you. In a combat zone, you have to be endlessly adaptable. Just dropped off to sleep when the Taliban decide to mortar you? Tough: adapt. Just come back from a hard patrol when you have to load up a QRF and go get some of your buddies in trouble? Tough: adapt. Find that the parameters of your mission have changed because someone much higher up the food chain than you has decided they should? Tough: adapt.

And this applies tenfold in the Special Forces. You go on a mission to lift a high-ranking enemy leader from a building where you're told he'll definitely be. You shoot your way in and find he's not there. What do you do? Lift some of the other people there in case they're useful? Take as much intel as you can find? Move on to another place nearby where you think he might be? All these decisions have to be made in seconds, and you have to factor in any number of considerations while doing so – how many people you've got the resources to detain, how much materiel you can carry, and so on. Whether you make the right or wrong decision is in some ways not the issue here. The issue is that you're adaptable enough to spin 180 on the hoof if need be and change your strategy around – you're not too hidebound in your thinking to follow a rigid game plan come what may.

Cycling fans saw a good example of this in the closing stages of the 2011 World Championships road race. Mark Cavendish was favourite to win, and with just over a kilometre to go he had two team-mates with him, Ian Stannard and Geraint Thomas. Stannard led the other two up the inside, but after Thomas had got through the gap the Aussie cyclist Matt Goss moved across just enough to cut Cavendish off and stop him from following his team-mates. In an instant Cavendish adapted to the new situation. He wouldn't be able to follow Stannard and Thomas anymore, so that option, Plan A, was gone. He knew Goss was in form and would be the man to beat anyway, so he tucked in behind him. A minute or so later they crossed the line: Cavendish first, Goss second. Cavendish's AQ had helped win him a world title.*

You need the kind of character which actually welcomes change rather than hides from it: you need to view your comfort zone as a place to get out of rather than a place to stay. Some people have a predominantly 'entity mindset', which means they believe that human attributes are fixed and can't be changed. Others have a predominantly 'incremental mindset', believing that

---

* His IQ also helped out here. Cavendish is famous for always doing a recce of his race finishes, either in person or via video link. He absorbs and processes a huge amount of information – gradients, corners, road width, traffic furniture, sightlines and so on – because he never knows which bits will be useful. In this race, the circuit looped around Copenhagen and the riders rode it multiple times. Each time Cavendish came down what would eventually be the finishing straight he noticed that the wind was gusting across from his right, pushing the riders left across the road. When it came to the final kilometre, he kept close to the right-hand barriers, taking the shortest route, in the knowledge that the wind would make the other riders drift left and open up a gap in front of him – which is exactly what happened.

those attributes can be changed through effort and hard work. Obviously, relatively few people are totally in one camp or the other, and for most people where you land is somewhere on a continuum; but the nearer you are to the incremental end, the better your AQ.

In the SAS my weeks were often very different from one day to the next, and I relished that. I could have spent Monday briefing government agencies about terrorist capabilities and locations, Tuesday doing weapons drills, Wednesday being briefed about the situation in the Middle East, Thursday jumping out of planes and Friday on my day off in B&Q getting some DIY stuff. Pivot, switch, adapt, flourish, day after day after day. Each of those are not just different activities requiring different skills, but also require shifts in mindset from one to the other, even between those which are ostensibly similar. There are differences between briefing government agencies and the situation in the Middle East. Same with weapons drills and parachuting: both needing attention to detail and constant repetition, but each taking place in very different environments.

Adaptability in warfare wasn't just a Western preserve, either. In fact, in some ways the Taliban were even more adaptable than we were, mainly because they had to be. They didn't have the technology or the equipment we did – no air support, no armoured vehicles, no massive ordnance – so they had to make the best of what they had, and they did that very well. IEDs are a case in point. Even the name, 'improvised explosive device', shows the innovation and adaptability which went into them. The Taliban were never going to win large-scale pitched battles against us, but by using IEDs they slowed down our patrols and locked in our resources when dealing with injured men or damaged equipment. Nor did they just keep churning out the same IEDs: they altered, developed and changed them, making them more powerful to blast through under-body armour (our blokes and the Americans started wearing armour plating between their legs to protect the old twig and berries) and even shitting on them before burying them in the dirt in order to increase the chances of secondary infection in anyone who got hit by one. We didn't like the Taliban, but we respected their fighting skills and the ways they kept causing us new and different problems. They were many things, but mugs they certainly weren't.

Adaptability has been around for as long as humans have; indeed, it's the key tenet of evolution itself. In *On the Origin of the Species*, the 1859 book which first propounded the theory of evolution, Charles Darwin wrote that 'it is not the strongest of the species that survives, nor the most intelligent: it is the one that is the most adaptable to change'. This applies across all species, and by extension all walks of human life, and so AQ is in many ways a broad church. It's not just about the capacity to absorb new information but also the willingness to unlearn obsolete knowledge (and of course the intelligence to know the difference.) In the 'leadership' section, I mentioned that some doctors and lawyers may soon be finding their jobs taken over by machines, especially those roles that involve spotting patterns in data (reviewing legal documents, diagnosing symptoms) as they can increasingly be done by computer algorithms. Algorithms are not going to get slower or weaker and human brains are not going to suddenly develop superpowers, so workers doing these jobs need AQ to survive. They have to accept that parts of their jobs will get hived off to machines, and to work on developing new skills which will not only enhance their jobs and add value to them, but also which they will be able to do better than machines. Creativity, lateral thinking and social skills are all still much more the preserve of man rather than machine, so those would be good areas to start – but not to finish. The options for change are constant both in breadth and depth. Learning to learn is mission critical, and this ability – not just to learn but to change, grow and experiment – will become far more important than mere narrow subject expertise.

Darwin spoke of species adapting to survive, but AQ is about thriving rather than simply surviving: about staying ahead of the curve, adapting to predict and influence change rather than just in response to it. The worst time to adapt is when you're told to, because by that time it's probably too late to do so properly and fully effectively. The best time to adapt is in advance of change – which, given that we can't know for sure exactly when that change will take place, means that the best time to adapt is always. Adaptation should be a constant process.

AQ is measured across three core dimensions which form the acronym ACE: ability, character and environment. *Ability* involves the adaptability skills themselves, *character* the aspects of your personality which lend themselves to fostering or rejecting the process of change, and *environment* the ways in which the same process is helped or hindered by external factors. Each dimension is divided into five sub-dimensions:

ABILITY

- *Grit*: the determination to push on without your commitment wavering.
- *Mental flexibility*: bending in response to unexpected developments, but never breaking and letting these developments derail you.

- *Mindset*: a healthy self-belief that this can be done.
- *Resilience*: recovering from setbacks.
- *Unlearning*: letting go of old skills and learning new ones.

I had to show all these during my move from 3 Para to the SAS. I was committed to the process, no matter how hard it might prove. I dealt with people dropping off Selection in a positive manner rather than by letting their weakness infect me; I absorbed their weakness and it gave me strength. David Goggins calls it taking souls: when you feel stronger because others are quitting or don't have the strength to continue. I always believed that I would make it, even when I was dog tired and hanging out of my arse; I kept going through injury which would have forced other people to withdraw; and when I passed and made it to The Regiment I realised that I would need to think for myself much more than I had done as a Para and not simply follow orders unquestioningly.

CHARACTER

- *Emotional range:* the extent to which you not just feel but welcome a variety of emotions, and the balance in your personality between positive and negative emotions.

- *Extraversion preference:* whether or not you're mainly extraverted or mainly introverted. Extraverts tend to score higher on AQ, though not always.
- *Hope:* AQ is at least partly founded on the hope that things will get better rather than worse, and that most progress is a good thing.
- *Motivation style:* AQ has to be collective to be effective – there's no point only one person or a handful of people changing if the rest of a large organisation remains stuck in its ways – and so those who might be more reluctant need to be persuaded and enthused that the ways forward really are beneficial.
- *Thinking style:* glass half-full or glass half-empty? Are you more inclined to look for reasons that things can be done or reasons that they can't?

I'm lucky in that my character is very suited to AQ, and I score well on all the above (as outlined in 'Self'). I embrace positive emotions, I'm an extravert, I'm an optimist (sometimes insanely so), I enjoy motivating those around me, and I always look for reasons to do things rather than not to.

ENVIRONMENT

- *Company support:* to what extent will your organisation support change?
- *Emotional health:* is the rest of your life in a good place to enable you to adapt, or are you so weighed down by external factors (sick family members, failing relationships, etc.) that you don't feel able to take risks?
- *Team support:* are the people immediately around you committed to change?
- *Work environment:* is this conducive to change? (This is a little different from 'company support' above. Company support is about whether the company is open to change; work environment is about whether that company has the capacity and systems in place to change effectively.)
- *Work stress:* are you spending so much time firefighting problems at work that there's no spare capacity there to consider longer-term strategy?

Since leaving the army I've deliberately put myself in environments which are conducive to adaptability and change. As my own boss I can not only support change but ensure I have the systems in place to make it happen. My personal life allows me to be adaptive and follow my own path, and if I do find myself getting bogged down in situations which are static or regressive I always have the option of walking out on them and cut myself free from being held back. This goes for life as well as just work: to progress as a person you have to put yourself, or be put into, uncomfortable situations, because only then do you see what you're really capable of. As the saying goes, 'Diamonds are made through pressure.' And how do you become a diamond as a person? Put yourself under pressure. Adaptability is pressure, otherwise there wouldn't be anything to adapt to. Keep an open mind so you see the world with fresh eyes and remain open to possibilities; an open heart so you can see situations through other people's eyes; and an open will so you can embrace the discomfort of the unknown.

INTELLIGENCE II: INFORMATION

Good intelligence is absolutely crucial in decision-making. The more information you have, the better your decision-making process will be, and that applies tenfold when the information you have is the right kind of information – that is, accurate, timely and germane to your needs. This has been the case for thousands of years. In the Bible, God tells Moses: 'Send some men to explore the land of Canaan. How many people are there and how strong are they? Are the towns fortified? Bring back examples of their fruits.' And Sun Tzu, the Chinese general whose *The Art of War* (written in about 500 BC) has been repurposed for the past 20 or 30 years as a business self-help book, wrote that 'what enables the wise sovereign and good general to strike and conquer and achieve things beyond ordinary men is foreknowledge'. Information is power, it's as simple as that – and the more good information, the greater the potential or actual power.

There are several methods of intelligence gathering in the military. One of the most important kinds is human intelligence; that is, intelligence gathered from other people. In your daily life you're unlikely to be listening in on intercepted phone calls or studying hi-res satellite images of secret nuclear facilities (and if you are then you've got the kind of job that you're not going to be telling too many people about), but you *are* likely to be coming across people every day who have information which you would find interesting, useful, or both.

Human intelligence was something we used pretty much every day in the army. When you're deployed in another country, you inevitably come across locals on a regular basis, and even though you're foreigners who are armed to the teeth and sweating buckets under 20 kg of body armour, you still look to make a connection with them (at least the ones who aren't actively trying to shoot you). You've come into their country and inserted yourself in their society, and inevitably you start to pick up information about that society: how it's organised, who has influence, who's allied with whom and who hates whose guts. (The latter two can change very fast in the Middle East: it's not uncommon to find two groups who were at each other's throats one day to be buddying up the next, usually against a common enemy.)

Anyone and everyone can be a source of intelligence if you know what you're looking for and how to get it out of them. In the army we had interpreters who obviously spoke the local language and dialect wherever we were, allowing them not just to listen in on Taliban radio comms (such as the incident I mentioned in 'Danger') but also to translate any conversations we had with the locals. We would talk to local government officials, tribal elders and ordinary citizens – market stall holders, taxi drivers, farmers. They all moved in different circles and all knew different things. Between them, we could build up a pretty accurate picture of what was going on.

Of course, they weren't all telling us the truth, and we weren't stupid enough to think that they were. Some of them would lie to us because they were covert supporters of the Taliban and wanted to feed us deliberate misinformation. Some would tell us things they genuinely thought were true but which were wrong, usually because they didn't know as much as they thought they did. And some would tell us what they thought we wanted to hear so as not to lose face or to befriend us. We had to work out which was which, by cross-referencing information back to intelligence we already had or by assessing the reliability of the various sources. A high-ranking official who demonstrably opposes the Taliban and has provided good intel on several previous occasions has earned the right to be taken seriously: a gobshite young kid who lies as easily as he breathes has to be treated as full of shit unless otherwise proven.

So how do you go about gathering intelligence in your day-to-day lives? To a large extent you're doing it already without realising, even if you might think of it as just harmless gossip! An awful lot of human conversation is about other humans, who may or may not be present at this conversation: mutual friends, current or former colleagues, people in the public eye, and so on. You talk about what people are up to: a promotion at work, a falling-out with a friend, an affair, a house or job move, kids and much else. This way you draw up a picture of people's lives, their triumphs and disasters, without thinking, and certainly without doing it in a structured way.

But say you have something specific in mind: nothing illegal, but something which is sensitive in some way, such as commercially. Go back to earlier in this chapter and the section on the seven questions as they applied to starting up ThruDark. Imagine you're starting a company and you need intelligence to help you make the best decisions possible. Of course you trawl the internet for any publicly available information, and there's a lot out there, but despite the grandest promises of technophiles the sum total of human knowledge is not yet just a Google search away. Most of the sum total of human knowledge is still where it's always been, in people's heads, and to get it out of there you have to know who to ask and what to ask them.

Before I went on Selection I got tips from some of the lads who'd done it before. As a result of what they told me, I turned up with a microwave so I could cook myself extra food – rice, bacon, tomato sauce, that kind of stuff. I got the piss ripped out of me, but I didn't give a fuck. Every day, before we began whichever hellish task lay ahead of us, I'd cook myself a bacon butty and pack it into my bergen. Out on the hills later that day, running on fumes and hanging out of my arse, I'd think, 'This is total shit, but you know what would make it a thousand times better? A bacon butty.' So I'd take my bergen off, sit down and spend five minutes savouring this butty. It was both a reward for keeping going, a pick-me-up to give more energy, and a warning – because when I'd finished it that was the time for me to tell myself, 'Right, stop being a twat and crack on.'

The good news is that most people love to talk about their jobs, unless their jobs are either exceptionally boring or exceptionally sensitive. And most people's default mode is to at least try to be helpful. So the most direct way, and one with a good chance of at least initial success, is to approach someone in the same industry and suggest having a coffee. There are plenty of conferences (or at least there were pre-Covid, and there will be again, even if more of them are virtual) where networking and meeting people is just as much the point as listening to the speakers or panel discussions. If you ask for a meeting with someone, chances are you'll get one, as long as you pitch yourself at the right level (e.g. don't think that if you're a junior associate fresh out of university you're going to get an hour's one-on-one with Apple CEO Tim Cook). Remember that a meeting is a two-way process, and that even if you're there to seek information from someone they will also be seeking something from you – information in return, perhaps, or the less tangible value of having another contact, or simply the ego boost of having their counsel sought.

At that meeting, have a list of questions you want to ask (and if you think that will make it too formal, then memorise them before you go in). There's no point coming out of there and only on the way home remembering a dozen things you should have asked. A follow-up e-mail asking for clarification on a couple of points is fine: a whole new tranche of questions makes you look like a rank amateur. If you get on well with the person then you may be able to make this a regular occasion, and depending on who they are – both their importance and their personality – you may get useful specifics out of them, or you may get generic information which you could have found anywhere. Remember your network is your net worth, so make sure you take it seriously and make sure you're bringing value to anything that you do, otherwise you won't get that second meeting. Relationships work both ways: if one person is bringing value and the other isn't, then that's not a relationship.

If you really want to collect information, then nothing beats doing it yourself; that is, going to work for a competitor and seeing how they do it. If you're starting out not just in this career but in your working life in general, this is a good way to go; indeed, you may not even have initially considered setting up on your own, being content to start with to work for someone else and learning the ropes. If you use your IQ to absorb the information coming in, your EQ to get on with your colleagues and encourage them to share their knowledge, and your AQ to apply these across as many different departments as possible, you'll gain a substantial amount of experience in no time.

The problem with working for a competitor is twofold. First, at any level beyond the most junior you'll probably have a no-compete clause in your contract, which forbids you from going to work for a competitor within a certain period of time after leaving this company. (In the City and some other industries this is called 'gardening leave', an enforced few months off between jobs while you wait out the no-compete period. Precious little gardening is done, and on City salaries it's usually someone else being paid to have green fingers anyway.) Second, to go and work for a competitor under false pretences – that is, not telling them that actually you have a company of your own in the same sector – is definitely unethical and in some circumstances illegal. The importance of integrity was always drummed into us both in the Green Army and the Special Forces. There are times when deception is necessary to save lives or to safeguard national security, but it's a lot harder to justify such deception when the reward might be an extra 2 per cent market share of widgets. There's a difference between being a hard businessman, even a ruthless one, and a deceitful one, and if they're honest most people know where that line lies.

When I went undercover as the mole on *SAS: Who Dares Wins*, I justified it to myself on two counts. First, all the contestants knew there'd be a mole, hence all the fruitless speculation in the first couple of days about who it was. They just didn't know the identity of that mole. Second, I was in there for a good reason, and that wasn't to grass people in it or get them in trouble with the DS for shits and giggles. It was to see from the inside who were the strong candidates and who weren't: to give the DS as much info as possible to do their jobs the best way they could. It was good to see, as a recruit, the people who wanted to be there at the end. That was something the DS didn't see. Having different access to the recruits was the whole point of the mole: looking for the well-rounded individual who pulled their weight when the DS weren't looking.

I won't deny that it was fun, though. It gave me something to occupy my mind with other than getting beasted, and sneaking around pretending to be someone else before feeding back intel under the other recruits' noses was exciting: it appealed to the inner 007 in me, and there's a reason why James Bond and other fictional spies are so popular. Going undercover and pulling off clandestine missions appeals to very deep parts of human nature: the need for thrills and the rush of outfoxing an opponent. There were no Aston Martins or bikini-clad supermodels on the Scottish hillsides, though, and in terms of real world intel that was all for the better. The reason I succeeded as a mole and didn't get my cover blown was that I deliberately made myself the grey man, determined not to stand out. Grey men aren't especially good or bad at anything: they're just so average that they fade into the background. I saw a similar thing on both P Company and Selection, even though neither of those involved moles. In both cases I'd been there a few weeks and the field was thinning out, and I saw blokes who must have been there the whole time but who I simply hadn't noticed until then. It's not that they'd gone out of their way to make themselves invisible – if someone does that then counter-intuitively it can be quite noticeable – but just that they'd naturally faded into the background. The grey men. Always there but never noticed.

People asked me whether I felt bad about betraying my fellow recruits, and the answer is no. I had a job to do and I did that job. Yes, I became friendly with a few, not just because I had to – making friends was all part of doing my job for my fellow DS, and I'd have stood out and potentially blown my cover if I hadn't gained any one's trust and befriended people – but also because I wanted to. I'm a sociable person by nature, certainly more sociable than I let myself be for those six days, and there were a couple of people like Ellie who I got close to. But I knew that when the truth came out that most people would take it in the right way and accept it as just part of the programme. It was no coincidence that the recruits I had most warmed to were among the ones who were strong enough mentally and physically to be there at the end. But at the end of the day I'd been a Special Forces operator for ten years, and I knew how to flick back into that role regardless of whether or not I liked a person or had built some kind of relationship with them. Ultimately we as the DS were there to test those recruits in every way possible and not to be their friends. And when I did reveal myself and began as an overt DS, the recruits showed me the same respect as they had done the other DS. I actually believe that they'd enjoyed or felt proud that they'd worked along-side me, and probably respected me even more as they knew what I was like as a recruit.

One of the things that I hope came across clearly on the programme was the importance not just of gathering information but also of using it correctly.

There are three stages to intelligence-gathering, and they're all as vital as each other: acquiring it, analysing it and applying it. They're three separate jobs and often require three separate people or groups of people to do each one. The agent who acquires the information doesn't need to know what that information will be used for, and doesn't necessarily know what will prove useful and what won't. Their job is just to acquire the information, which often takes days, weeks or even months of questioning. That information then goes to the analyst, who will be collating information from many different sources. It's the analyst who should be able to discern patterns in what they're seeing, find meaning in apparently random small bits of information, and be able to put together these pieces and patterns in the same way they might find which jigsaw pieces fit together or how getting one crossword clue right gives enough information to get another one right, and so on. And from the analyst it goes to the people in the field or in enforcement capacities who can actually act on that information: police officers making arrests, for example, or surveillance operatives sent to observe new targets, or the redeployment of specialist resources.

One of the things which gets most attention on *SAS: Who Dares Wins* is the polar opposite of intelligence-gathering; that is, interrogation and resistance to it. There are plenty of reasons for people's fascination with this, and very little is to do with how likely you are in civilian life to be subject to proper interrogation techniques (unless you count a livid spouse yelling, 'Where are the passports? WHERE ARE THE FUCKING PASSPORTS?' when you're in the queue at Gatwick and realise you left them on the kitchen table). I think people are interested because they want to see how long recruits can last without breaking, because there's something horrifying about some of the more extreme techniques used (they're not used by the British army on foreign nationals), and also because it's instructive to see that actually sometimes it's the softness that finishes you off rather than the hardness; that someone being polite and kind can kick away the last of your defences more effectively than all the ranting, raving and threats of violence which have come before.

If you do ever find yourself being properly interrogated, the following ten tips will help you:

1. Under the Geneva Convention, you are only obliged to give an interrogator four items of information: name, rank, army number and date of birth. But if that means being shot in the head because you're no good to them, then it's time to leak out some information that isn't going to put anyone's life at risk.

2. Kindness and gentle questioning can be more effective than harsh interrogation, so beware. It's not just the

relief you might feel when someone stops yelling at you: it's that all our normal social interactions revolve around basic friendliness, and it's very hard to switch that off. If someone asks you whether you want a cup of tea, or if it's better with the light turned down like that, or any other of a thousand everyday innocuous questions, it feels weird to respond either with silence or with your name, rank, army number and date of birth. But it's what you have to do.

3. The interrogators will try to form some sort of rapport with you, whether that's based on fear or some kind of common ground – football, travel, films, whatever. Again, the temptation to discuss these things is almost overwhelming, and again you have to resist it.

4. The good cop/bad cop duality is well known, but in fact skilled interrogators may take on up to four different roles (though obviously more than one can be played by the same person). There's the good cop: kind, friendly, understanding and persuasive. There's the bad cop: threatening, insulting and sarcastic. But there's also the cold, apparently unfeeling interrogator who just asks questions relentlessly and monotonously, showing neither compassion nor animosity; and there's the questioner who seems naïve and credulous to the point of believing you're

innocent, but who is of course trying to lull you into a false sense of security and make you slip up through complacency.

5. Knowing in advance some of the psychological tricks they're likely to use - shining a light in your face and speaking from behind it so you can't see their faces, putting you on an uncomfortable chair, forcing you to strip and then telling you what a small cock you have, and so on - will give you a small sense of victory when they use them: a bit of, 'Oh, right on cue, lads. Haven't you got anything better than that old chestnut?' It may only be a small victory and an inward smirk, but in interrogation scenarios you take your wins when and where you find them.

6. There's a reason why those four pieces of information are the only words you should say: anything else can be edited into a video or audio tape to make it sound like you said something you didn't. Even a simple 'yes' or 'no' - in fact, even a nod or a shake of the head - can be spliced in after a totally unrelated question, perhaps even one asked by someone you've never met. If you answer 'yes' to the question 'Would you like a cup of tea?', that 'yes' can be made to look as though you agreed with a statement denouncing British foreign policy or criticising the government,

which in turn will be a propaganda victory for the enemy. And certainly don't sign anything.

7. As with being a mole, be the grey man. The quicker and more effectively you can convince your interrogators that you're no one special and have no information worth the name, the safer you'll be and the quicker you're likely to be released. Shouting 'Fuck you!' and trying to swing a punch at your captors might make you feel better for a few seconds, but it's just going to make life much harder for you further down the line. There's no one around to be impressed by your defiance, so save it. But by the same token there's no mileage in fawning, grovelling or abasing yourself either: this will make your interrogators question you even harder, either because this kind of behaviour has pissed them off or because they think you're trying to hide something.

8. Eat, drink and go to the toilet whenever you're offered the chance. You never know how long it will be before the opportunity comes again. And don't be shy to ask for these things: shy kids don't get sweets, and food and water might be the only things that can keep you alive.

9. Torture is unknown territory for most people, and it's impossible to know how you'll react until it happens to you. There are two main reasons the British army

don't use it, one moral and the other practical. First, it's barbaric, and the army prides itself on not only defending our way of life but also doing it in a way which is consistent with our national values. Second, it doesn't work. Oh, most people will eventually confess if they're subject to enough mental or physical pressure, but the value of what they confess is likely to be more or less worthless. People will say anything to make pain stop if that pain gets bad enough. The whole point of interrogation is not to get the prisoner to confess in and of itself: it's to get him to tell the truth, for that truth to have intelligence value, and for the flow of information to be continuous and extensive rather than brief, confined and one-off. Most likely the country or organisation that have you want to use you as some kind of political puppet, so parading you on TV with a missing eye and covered in blood will only make them look barbaric.

10. Take yourself away mentally as much as you can. Anytime you're not being asked questions, just switch off. It'll help to ease the pain, whether that pain is physical (being put in stress positions) or mental (being played footage of children screaming), and it will also save your concentration for when you need it, during the interrogation itself. Batsmen in Test

cricket switch off between every delivery, letting their minds wander or go blank until it's time to focus again. Concentrating hard when you don't have to is a surefire way to burn through your energy and weaken your defences at a time when you'll most need them. Let them control your body if they want, but make sure your mind remains yours and yours alone. The moment they get control of your mind is the moment they've broken you.

EXCELLENCE

Excellence is not a singular act. It's a habit.
You are what you repeatedly do.

Shaquille O'Neal

The relentless pursuit of excellence is one of the four key tenets of the SAS. What's interesting about that phrase 'the relentless pursuit of excellence' is that each part is equally important. It would have been easy enough just to say 'excellence' and leave it at that. After all, shouldn't excellence be an ideal in most walks of life? If something's worth doing then it's worth doing properly, surely.

Well, yes and no. Of course it should be an ideal, but if excellence were easy then it wouldn't be excellence. Which is where the 'relentless pursuit' bit comes in. Calling it a pursuit shows that excellence isn't something which just happens, or even something which is an inevitable by-product of hard work or a certain level of attainment. Excellence is elusive and rarefied: it needs to be chased, hunted, wrestled and pinned down. And this is not a pursuit which can be done lightly or only when you feel like it. This has to be less an action that you take than a state of mind: that everything you do is geared at getting better, no matter how small or insignificant those things might seem. You do not let up, not for a second. You are relentless, because you have to be. You never stop, because excellence doesn't stand still. Standards are always rising. What was excellent today will be merely acceptable tomorrow; what was acceptable today won't be good enough tomorrow. You can never rest on what you have achieved in the past. You always have to improve.

The SAS wears its excellence in a very understated way, a rather British way. We call ourselves 'The Regiment'. There are no others. I like the simplicity of that: so self-assured that we didn't need to qualify it with anything else. I know the word 'special' is part of the official name – Special Air Service, Special Forces – but I've always felt a little uncomfortable with that. 'Special' is a little misleading. It can make us sound as though we're superhuman or invulnerable, and we're not, not in the slightest. The moment you think you're special is the moment complacency begins to set in. I never once felt when going into contact with, for example, the Taliban: 'Oh fine, I'm special, me, who the fuck do these blokes think they are? We'll fucking mop 'em up for even daring to step to us.' If I had felt that I'd have probably got a bullet in my head, and I'd have equally probably deserved it for being such a twat. No: I never felt I was special. I was just doing my job to a very high standard, a very high standard indeed. It was the same job I'd been doing since I first signed up for the Paras as that scrawny 19-year-old. It was just that now I was doing it a million times better than I'd been doing to start with. I was doing it with excellence. That's all.

There are four main aspects to the pursuit of excellence: professionalism, people, preparation and pride. *Professionalism* is doing everything as well as you can possibly do. *People* are those around you who inspire and teach you. *Preparation* is not just training but the willingness to make mistakes and learn from them. *Pride* is the sense of belonging to a group which is of the highest quality and intends to remain that way.

PROFESSIONALISM

Professionalism is about doing everything right, no matter how small or insignificant that may be. It's easy and tempting to slack on the little things, but if you do that then sooner or later you'll be tempted to slack on the big things. How we do anything is how we do everything. It's the 'broken windows theory', first proposed by James Wilson and George Kelling in 1982: if a broken window is left unrepaired then the rest of the windows in the building will soon be broken, as it's a sign that no one cares enough to fix them. In the 1990s Rudy Giuliani and William Bratton, mayor and police commissioner respectively of New York City, decided to tackle the city's atrocious crime rate by following this theory. They clamped down on crimes so small as to seem almost insignificant in the great swathes of a vast, teeming city. Vandalism, loitering, public drinking, jaywalking, fare evasion and the like: these were suddenly all fair game for the police, to the astonishment and dismay of the thousands who'd been doing them with impunity for years. And, in general, it worked: violent crime in New York City dropped by 56 per cent during the 1990s, double the national rate.*

* The zero tolerance campaign wasn't the only reason for the fall, and not all the methods used were beyond reproach – most notably, the NYPD's relationship with poor black communities was no better than in many other big cities, with many cases of police brutality and racism – but in terms of what Giuliani and Bratton had set out to do, which was to make the city as a whole a much nicer place in which to live, the programme was an emphatic success.

That's why I looked after the little details. If you keep your eye on the ball there then you'll do it with the big things. The army is very hot on professionalism, of course. In the Green Army at least you have to make your bed so well that you could bounce a coin off the sheets, and polish your boots until you can see your face in them, and make sure there's not a speck of dust anywhere in your room. When you're a brand new recruit and the corporals come to do their inspection, they'll always find something that's not up to standard, and then everyone gets beasted for it. Some people outside the army don't understand the point of this, and think it's stupid: what does it matter if you haven't dusted everywhere, and why does everyone get punished rather than just the person whose mistake it was? The answer is professionalism: you need to maintain your standards in every area as you never know which one will count, and the 'you' there is a collective not a singular one. Any outfit, not just an army, is only as professional as its least professional member.

For example, when I was doing the two big selection courses, P Company to be a Para and Selection itself for the SAS, I'd put my bergen out the night before (having weighed it to make sure it was the right weight for the next day's task) and then I'd sleep in my kit. It just meant there was less to do the following morning so I could stay in bed longer, not through laziness but because I needed all the sleep and rest I could get. If you have to get up at 5 a.m., why get up at four just to unload everything from your bergen and then load it again just to be sure you've got everything you need? Sounds insane, right? Yet that's what a lot of blokes did: banging around the dorm before it was even light outside, making more noise than the fucking brass band of the Blues and Royals, and getting themselves in a stew about whether they'd left anything behind. Guess what? Those fuckers never passed. Not one of them.

The same applied the night before. You'd get lads who'd stay up late stretching out on foam rollers so as to be ready for the exercise the next day. But when you've got six hours of sleep in between you stretching and the exercise starting, that's only going to be of limited use. I'd stretch when I got back, no matter how exhausted I was. Blokes would be flopping around and moaning about how tough it was: that for me was just wasted time. Get back in, run cold water on your legs to flush out the lactic, stretch out, and from then on in everything is rest. On those courses you need only two things when you're not being beasted: calories and rest. I'd microwave my rice and chow down as much as I could. I was resting physically, and I was also resting mentally as I'd done everything I needed to do, and so didn't have to worry about that either. It was really very simple, but you'd be surprised how many people made it unnecessarily complex. That's another thing about being professional: nine times out of ten it's the simplest and most obvious course that's the best. Not always, of course, and certainly not on complex and risky SAS ops, but when you're hammering yourself for a week flat then yes, most definitely. As the old acronym goes: KISS. Keep it simple, stupid.

Even though I'm not especially one for routine in general, as evidenced by the variety I like to have in my life, I still like to have a routine, if that makes sense. By having a routine in small things it allows me not to have a routine in larger things, because I know I have my baselines covered. Think of a plane. It has wings for when it's in the air, but it also has wheels for when it's on the ground. Those wheels are the least glamorous and exciting part of a plane, but they're just as vital as anything else – without them the plane can't take off, land, taxi or manoeuvre – and so they need to be maintained. Maintaining the wheels – taking care of the boring stuff – was for me the essence of professionalism.

And that's not just because the boring stuff underlays everything else, but because enough little things done well end up forming big things done well. This is marginal gains, as pursued by pretty much every top sports team for the past decade or two: an aggregate of small gains which by themselves don't make much difference but which when put together can be decisive. Take the Canadian hurdler Mark McKoy, who I mentioned in 'Self'. His hurdling technique used to be flawed. His lead leg over the hurdle was nice and straight as it should have been, but his trail leg was pointing slightly outwards, so that when that foot next hit the track it wasn't quite properly aligned and cost him a tiny bit of forward momentum. His coach noticed this and made him practise and practise until that trail leg came through dead straight. It saved him an inch of distance every time he did it, and he did it 39 times a race.

He won the 1992 Olympics by 39 inches.

Clearly soldiering doesn't always lend itself to such precise correlations between input and output, but the principle remains the same. You do everything you can because in the end it will add up. You set yourself, or are set, goals for every training session you do. Say I'm working with a new sniper rifle. I can go through the motions, take a few shots, read the manual, play around with the features and generally look as though I'm doing something useful. Or I can say to myself: right, you're not wrapping up this session until you've hit the centre of a target at 800 metres distance five times in a row. The first option will bring some benefit – it's better than nothing – but the second is exponentially better, because you've demonstrably improved by the end of the session in relation to where you'd been at the start. The true professional never looks at any kind of training exercise as something merely to turn up and do: he always looks at it as an opportunity to improve. And if that exercise doesn't offer that opportunity, then go and do one that does. Marathon runners can face the same problem when they run 'junk miles': they're getting miles in their legs, but they're basically plodding along without stretching themselves, without varying pace or effort or anything which might help them get fitter and faster. They're plateauing, basically: not necessarily losing fitness or speed, but not gaining it either. Professionals never plateau. The phrase 'that'll do' will never do.

This refusal to plateau comes through in other ways too. You have to be self-critical and honest with yourself (which relates back to EQ in 'Intelligence'). The honest professional sees clearly where they've fallen short and not only pledges to do better, but follows a plan to do so. A professional doesn't make excuses, because a professional wants results. You can have excuses or results, but not both. Again, you see this mindset in top-level sportsmen, who won't blame anything but themselves, even when they could reasonably point to certain factors – luck, chance, fate – having gone against them. The reason they won't look to those things for excuses is nothing to do with whether they might have a reason to do so in any particular instance. It's because the moment you shift ownership of your performance onto something or someone else even once, you'll be more tempted to do it next time round.

The flipside is that to be properly professional you have to be given the right tools too. You can't give someone a pistol, ask them to hit that sniper target 800 metres away that I mentioned and then blame them when they can't do it. I've been in situations when I haven't been given the tools to do the job I was there to do, whether that was inadequate equipment or being hamstrung by political considerations, and believe me it's embarrassing. You're sitting around like a lemon, desperate to get on with things but unable to do so through no fault of your own. It's the worst of both worlds, and reflects badly both on you and whoever you work for. Either let someone do a job and equip them properly for it, or bug out. For operational reasons I can't and don't want to say when and how this happened to me, but here are a couple of public domain examples from Bosnia before my time in the army: the Dutch UN peacekeepers who were totally ill-equipped to stop the 1995 Srebrenica massacre or the British soldiers attached to UNPROFOR who weren't allowed to remove civilians from dangerous areas for their own protection as that would have been deemed assisting in ethnic cleansing.

PEOPLE

Much of my desire to be excellent came from seeing people around me, particularly those who were already where I wanted to be. There was a time when I was overseas with 3 Para and some lads from the SBS invited us over for a game of volleyball – just like *Top Gun*, except with fewer cheesy eighties tracks and much less by way of homoerotic overtones. They hadn't been doing much and we'd been getting into quite a few scraps, so they wanted to hear all about them.

It's hard to overstate how much of an aura Special Forces lads have around them when you're a private on your first tour. It wasn't just that the SBS lads looked different, with their beards and kit that was visibly better than ours; it was also the way they carried themselves. They were a breed apart and they knew it. Like I said earlier, 'special' doesn't mean superhuman, just exceptionally good at what they do, and these lads were certainly that. Wherever they went, you knew who they were without needing to ask or be told. It reminded me of that barbecue scene in *Black Hawk Down* when Steele, a captain in the Rangers, approaches Hoot, a sergeant first class in Delta Force, points to Hoot's gun and says: 'Delta or no Delta, that's a hot weapon [i.e. loaded]. You know better than that. Your safety should be on at all times on base.' Hoot wriggles his index finger and replies, 'Well, this is my safety, sir.' It wasn't that the SBS boys behaved exactly like that (and in fact I doubt that scene was especially true to life, both in terms of safety precautions and of a sergeant talking to a superior officer like that, irrespective of Special Forces status); it was more that they weren't bound by all the regulations that we were.

The other thing which really impressed me about them was what good blokes they were. I'd expected them to be arrogant and really up themselves, but they weren't at all. They were confident, sure, but they were also really friendly, they treated all of us just the same as they treated each other, and in general they were very humble and down to earth. If anything they were even more so than some of those in the Green Army, and it took me a while to work out why. It was, of course, because these guys didn't have anything to prove. When you're the best you don't need to go running around telling everyone that you're the best.

I wanted a piece of all that. I wanted to be one of them. Lots of people didn't: there were plenty of my fellow Paras who were happy just to be Paras, even though in some ways the Paras and the Marines are sort of halfway houses between the Special Forces and the regular infantry, so it was quite a natural jumping-off point if you wanted a crack at Selection. These SBS guys with their beards and their kit and their sense of freedom were role models for me. I never had role models when growing up. I was a kid in Preston who'd spend my weeks at a school I hated or a job which bored me, and my weekends getting pissed in the park on cider with my mates. I had no one to really inspire me, no one whose example I could point to and say, 'Yes, this is how I want to live my life.'

Role models are critical when it comes to seeking out excellence. Excellence is all about having standards to aim at, and seeing people who are living those standards already is very powerful. One of the things I most like about *SAS: Who Dares Wins* is that it provides those role models. People look at the instructors and me and see things in us to admire. This doesn't mean we're perfect, far from it – you'd go a long way to find five less perfect blokes! – but we *have* done stuff which has tested us, made us better people and forged us with good values. In a world where people are sitting at home bleaching their hair and staring at their phones for hours on end, it can be hard to find decent role models, especially for men. Yes, you have footballers, especially lads like Marcus Rashford with his campaign for free school meals, who do some real good for society, but who else? *Love Island*? Do me a favour. That's all about how you look, and though all those blokes go to the gym like fiends and have their six-packs and all that, deep down they're soft as shit. I don't mean that to be as critical as it might sound. They're soft because they've never had reason not to be, and that goes for most people in society. It's that old saying: hard times produce hard men, hard men produce soft times, soft times produce soft men, soft men produce hard times, and round it goes again. I needed hard men as role models, and I found them. I hope that my example inspires people to go after their own version of excellence; that for me would be as much of a triumph as passing Selection or climbing Everest, that I had passed on some of the good that was passed on to me.

PREPARATION

You know the old army adage: 'Fail to prepare, prepare to fail.' And to a large extent it's true. Preparation is one of the bedrocks of excellence. If you just turn up and wing something, chances are it'll all go to shit unless it's so easy that anyone could do it. I can't think of a single difficult thing I did that I hadn't prepared for thoroughly beforehand. It's the reason that the SAS train so hard and why they stress test operational plans so heavily: the more you prepare, the less there is to go wrong, or perhaps more accurately the less there is to go wrong that you haven't foreseen. Things will always go wrong.

But to see failure as the flip side of preparation is not all that helpful either. First, just as many things end in failure as success, if not more so, no matter how much you prepare for them. Second, failure is only a bad thing if you don't learn from it. The only way not to fail is not to try in the first place. Pretty much every major scientific discovery has come after strings of failures, and often the breakthroughs have been more or less accidental. Fall seven times, get up eight. Failure is nothing to be scared of. Failure is an inevitable stepping stone on the way to excellence. You must learn to fail before you learn to succeed. What's even more powerful is if you find something that scares you even more that failure; for me I fear boredom and living a dull life way more than I fear failure.

My abortive attempt to climb Manaslu is a perfect example of this. We made so many mistakes and prepared so badly that it was almost embarrassing.

Failure on this trip was not just almost inevitable but in the end a good thing, because if we'd got to the top after all that had gone wrong it might have given us an inflated sense of our own climbing skill – 'We did so much wrong and we still got away with it, we must be the dog's bollocks' – and that in itself would have been very dangerous further down the line.

What were our fuck-ups? God, where do you start? We flew out way too late, three weeks after we should have done, which in a climbing window of only six weeks halved our available time and meant that we had to rush acclimatisation. That had a knock-on effect on everything else. Because we hadn't acclimatised properly when we started to climb up to Camp 1 it was much harder than it should have been. It's normally five hours, but in the end it took us eight or nine, and I was suffering like a dog. I remember leaning on my poles, sucking in air and trying to get even a small amount of rest, but knowing that if I sat down for so much as a minute I'd find it almost impossible to get up again. I had that little nugget of ego – you're the mountain guide, pull yourself together, crack on, don't be the twat – but I didn't even know that I wasn't properly acclimatised, as this was the first 8,000-metre mountain I'd been on, which was another mistake: I'd gone from climbing in the Alps and Dolomites straight to here, and though some of those mountains had been technically difficult, they just didn't compare in terms of altitude.

Then when it came to push for the summit, I decided to weigh my food out and take as little of it as possible so as to save weight. Big mistake. Huge mistake. In the high reaches of a Himalayan mountain you need all the energy you can get; the extra weight of the food is nothing compared to how fucked you are without enough fuel. It's always better to take too much food rather than too little. We were caught in a snowstorm on the way up to Camp 2, and so we had to bunk up with some German guys I knew from the mountain course who were also delayed on their summit push. There were three of us in a two-man tent with all our equipment, so it was cosy to say the least – luckily this was pre-Covid, as we certainly wouldn't have passed social distancing rules – and the storm was bad enough to keep us there for two days, which of course meant that I ran out of food. Luckily, and inevitably, the Germans had come better prepared and gave me some of theirs, but still. This had a massive knock-on effect on my energy levels.

Basically, we had done what no mountaineers should ever do, and left ourselves no safety margins whatso-ever. So much can go wrong on mountains that you have to build in a whole load of slack, and we hadn't even begun to do that. So when on day three the storm had passed, the skies were blue and it looked a perfect day to push for the summit, I was absolutely fucked. I hadn't eaten enough, I hadn't acclimatised well enough, and we had to try for the summit now or lose the window for good. In the end, as I said in 'Danger', I feared that if I continued to climb upwards I might get caught in an avalanche – I might even have triggered one myself – and pretty much the only sensible decision I took on that entire mountain was to shitcan the chance of summiting and head back down the slopes.

So a total failure, sure. But also a failure from which I could learn lots of lessons, if only I was prepared to take them: if I was prepared to subsume my ego in the quest for excellence. I *did* take them, and as a result my first ascent of Everest was almost ridiculously smooth. Yes, I got lucky with conditions and the like, but I also put myself in the best position to exploit them by doing the things Manaslu had taught me: acclimatisation, nutrition, safety margins. All the things I got right on Everest were the things I'd got wrong on Manaslu. The road towards excellence is not just a steep one but a winding one too, as the Beatles almost sang.

PRIDE

Excellence is a collective concept as much as an individual one.

Any regiment worth its salt takes great pride in not just its current status but its history too – the wars it's been deployed to, the battles it has fought, the medals its men have received. The Americans were big on this in both Iraq and Afghanistan: you could hardly walk into one of their briefing rooms or chow halls without seeing unit flags, battle streamers and the like. I would look at the list of sergeant majors in Hereford, and while I personally knew the incumbent, and the couple before him too, seeing those names stretching right back to 1942 connected me to the history of the place. The three sergeant majors I knew had known the three sergeant majors before them, and so on all the way back to the start. Those men had looked after men like me who'd fought in Malaya, and Oman, and Aden, and Ulster, and Bosnia, and a whole heap of other places besides on missions so hush-hush that only a handful of people knew about them. They had served The Regiment with distinction. When you go to the Special Forces Club in London, there are photos of members all the way up the stairs, with short pieces of text detailing who they are and what they've done. Black frames round the photos means they're dead; silver ones are for those still alive. All this kind of thing makes me proud to be a part of something with such a glorious history, and proud to have played my own small part in keeping that going: that in years to come I would be part of the fabric to some keen young troopers just as those old-timers were part of the fabric to me.

You can see the same thing in some sports teams: national football, cricket and rugby teams assign each player a number, which is not the one on the back of their shirt but the one above their heart. It's their cap number: 482 means that you're the 482nd person to play for your country, and that connects you to all the people who've played before you and all those who'll come after you too. The British & Irish Lions go one further. Before a match, they'll put three names above the changing slot of each player: great players of the past who've represented the Lions in the same position. The message is simple: these are the boots you're filling, this is the company you're keeping, don't let them down. We humans are tribal animals, and to feel part of something bigger than ourselves is a very powerful driving force.

When the past is held up as excellence, that excellence becomes the standard for all to pursue, and in doing so every individual holds not just themselves but also each other to that level. If you're part of a group which aspires towards and achieves excellence, then that makes it easier for you to find excellence on a personal level. Being part of that group, and being proud to be part of that group, ensures not only that you have people around you from whom you can seek advice and help, but also that you don't want to be the one who lets the side down. This in turn means that the leader doesn't have to keep on at his men to achieve more. If there's proper collective pride, the team polices itself, and ensures that anyone who slacks off either improves or is removed. People aren't late to meetings and don't forget gear. They pay attention during meetings and do whatever needs to be done rather than waiting for someone else to do it.

Pride begets excellence, and that excellence continues the tradition of not just having things to be proud of but earning them too – for excellence has to be earned, or else it isn't excellence. Every unit which has a storied history began somewhere, with no history, no battle trophies, no medals and no citations. They all earned those things the hard way, by pushing their men and testing them until they achieved things which required unity, strength and perseverance. As former SEAL commander Jocko Willink says, 'If you want to build pride, you have to bring pain. Pride comes from shared suffering. Sure, pride comes from history, and pride comes from winning, but you can't count on that. If you want your team members to have pride, you have to make them earn it through hard work.'

The point about being tribal animals also means that we seek both pride and excellence not just in themselves but also in relation to other people. If you think one nation's army likes to compare itself with another's, rest assured that the rivalry is nothing compared to that between different regiments in that army. In the Vietnam War, an Aussie major called Harry Smith was in command of Delta Company, 6th Royal Australian Regiment. He was determined to make Delta the best Aussie company in Vietnam.

Where the battalion specified ten kilometres, Harry ordered twelve. Where it specified fifteen-kilo packs, Harry ordered twenty-kilo packs. Where an activity specified sandshoes, Harry ordered boots and gaiters; this was to strengthen the legs and general fitness needed in battle. Delta came to be the fittest, fastest, most tactically proficient, most secure company in the battalion. On every exercise, it seemed that Delta got the outside leg of the sweep, forcing them to move further and faster than anyone else. Delta simply relished the task. By now, all the faint hearts and weak minds had joined the coughers and farters in some other location and Delta was a company confident in any task.*

In August 1966 Delta would end up fighting the Battle of Long Tan, which is to the Aussies what Rorke's Drift is to us: a tale of scarcely believable heroism against overwhelming odds. In a monsoon-lashed rubber plantation, 200 Delta soldiers held off 2,000 Viet Cong for all of an afternoon and part of a night. It was the excellence of Delta's soldiering which not only saved them but saw them triumphant. If Harry Smith hadn't been so determined to make Delta better than all the other companies there, his men would almost certainly have been wiped out.

From the moment I joined the Paras, it was drummed into me that this was the best regiment in the army, or at least the Green Army. (We did actually think we were better than the Special Forces, but we obviously weren't.) Everything we did was designed to reinforce a simple mantra: we are by far the best infantry force in the army, we're the hardest, and everyone else is a fucking screamer. Even our barracks – Helles, in Catterick

---

* Robert Grandin, *Danger Close: The Battle of Long Tan.*

– bore this out. Other units – normal units – had duvets, posters, TVs, that kind of stuff, like it was some sort of holiday camp. But we had bare walls and itchy blankets and no creature comforts. It was spartan, deliberately so. We loved it. We didn't need anything that might make us soft. Everything we could do to make us feel harder we did, and that meant that we kept upping our standards.

The Paras' biggest rivalry is with the Marines. This is understandable, as they're both cut from the same cloth – as I said, both are sort of halfway houses between the regular infantry and the Special Forces. The rivalry is intense and runs deep, but in general it's a good thing. A Para and a Marine will argue till the cows come home about which of their Selection procedures is tougher, P Company or the Marines' Commando Course. When blokes were coming back from Afghanistan having lost limbs to IEDs, they were taken to the Defence Medical Rehabilitation Centre (DMRC) at a place called Headley Court in Surrey, where they'd be fitted with prosthetics and taught to walk again. As you can imagine, it was a tough process in every way: young men who'd been at the peak of physical fitness, doing a job they loved, now having to adjust to life as amputees.

But the physios found something very revealing: when a Para and a Marine were in rehab together, they would strive with everything they had to recover quicker than the other. If the doctors said they'd be able to walk again in four weeks, they'd be determined to do it in two. There'd be a couple of nutters, one in a maroon T-shirt and the other in a laurel green one, absolutely determined to beat the other back to being able to walk normally. The rivalry drove both sides on to achieve things others had thought impossible. There was a lighter side too, in the form of a maroon T-shirt which said on the front 'God is a Para' beneath our regimental cap badge – and only when you turned it over did you see that on the back was written, 'but only because he failed the Commando Course'.

Fucking Marine screamers.

The same kind of rivalry also feeds through into the one between the SAS and the SBS, the Special Boat Service. (There's obviously some connection with Paras and Marines too: just by the nature of the regimental specialities, more Paras tend to go to the SAS and more Marines to the SBS.) The SAS/SBS rivalry is also dictated by geography, strange as that may sound. The SAS is based in Hereford, which is real farming country, so you get a certain vibe from all that: tractors, field sports and wax jackets. The SBS is based on the coast and so there's a very different vibe there: more surfing, sailing and posh beach-side houses.

But unlike the Marines and the Paras, the SBS has always been publicly seen in the shadow of the SAS. This is nothing to do with how good the SBS operators are, because they're top class, as soldiers, guys and as a unit. It's all to do with history and public image. Everyone knows the SAS, and in fact the SAS have been credited with quite a bit of stuff that was actually the SBS. Even the letters, A and B, in our names tend to suggest that the SAS are just that little bit better. Whether we are or not depends on who you ask, but three things are for sure: that if one or other is better it's not by much; that the rivalry is in general pretty good-natured because we all understand that we're on the same side at the end of the day; and most of all that any army in the world would bite their hand off to have two Special Forces regiments as good as the ones we have.

RESILIENCE

Do not judge me by my success. Judge me by how
many times I fell down and got back up again.

Nelson Mandela

Resilience is one of the key ingredients for success in life, let alone soldiering. Sooner or later everyone faces setbacks, disappointments, trauma and tragedy. No one gets through life unscathed – they just don't. And while it's easy to cope when life is good, it's how you deal with things when they go to shit which not only defines how resilient you are but how you are as a person in general. Only when you put people through the fire do you see what they're really made of.

There's a lot of talk these days about mental health, particularly among soldiers; certainly much more talk than there used to be, but perhaps still not as much talk as there should be. Resilience is a key aspect of mental health. It's also a reminder that mental health is something positive rather than just an absence of negatives. It's not simply a question of having no disorders or problems, any more than physical health is a question of having no illness or injuries. Resilience is not freedom from suffering difficulty, distress, emotional pain or sadness – quite the opposite. It's experiencing one, more or all of these things and getting through them. There's no resilience needed to travel down a smooth road.

And to be honest, I'm grateful for the times I've needed to call on my resilience, because those times have reminded me that everything in life is about balance. Without the darkness I wouldn't appreciate the light, without the sadness I wouldn't appreciate the joy, without pushing myself to my limits I wouldn't appreciate lying on a beach. Life is yin and yang, and neither exists without the other. As the ancient Greek philosopher Socrates said, the unexamined life is not worth living.

It's tempting to think of resilience as something innate, a quality you either have or you don't. While it's true that some people are more naturally resilient than others, it's also true that resilience can be learned, practised, enhanced and improved, whoever you are and wherever you're starting from. Writing yourself or others off as not being resilient is a cop-out. The whole ethos behind soldiering, an ethos which I've always tried to carry through to life in general, is that you can always improve in any field. The only difference between practising resilience and practising, for example, weapons drills is in the nature of what's being practised, not the practice itself. The alternative is that you dwell too long and too much on the negative consequences of trauma or stress. Resilience is a skill, and like all skills it can be cultivated and nurtured.

Think of playing the guitar. Pretty much everyone who starts out gets sore fingers, and for some that's enough to make them quit after only a few lessons. But the resilient person continues to practise because he knows the end result will be worthwhile. The more he practises, and the more his fingers get used to the demands of playing, the tougher and stronger they become, which enables him to practise more. It's a virtuous circle: his fingers become more resilient as a result of practice, which in turn enables him to keep improving. The increasing strength in his fingers, and their enhanced ability to withstand pain, have a direct and positive effect on the standard of his play.

The fingers are resilience; the playing is life.

So what goes into being resilient? Some of it is stuff I've already discussed in previous chapters. Having good EQ, for a start: a strong baseline of emotional wellbeing, the ability to recognise and manage your own emotions, and a solid network of people you trust can all help when things get rough. Having good AQ is also vital. We need resilience when things change for the worse, and so being able to cope with change, to look for the positives and to see opportunities through the darkness are also critical here.

But these are only starting points. I've found over the years that my own resilience can be summed up in seven 'V's: values, validation, viewpoint, variant, vehemence, viability and visualisation.

- *Values* are my core values, the things I hold dearest in terms of the way I want to live my life and which remain constant no matter what else is going on around me.
- *Validation* is reminding myself of past successes and examples of resilience, which help reassure me that since I've got through them then I can get through this too.
- *Viewpoint* is seeing the situation in the round and getting perspective on it, which is especially useful when what's in front of me can seem overwhelming.
- *Variant* is the recognition that when it comes to coping methods there's no one-size-fits-all answer:

what works for me may not work for other people and vice versa, and indeed what worked for me in the past may not work for me now and in the future.

- *Vehemence* is the intensity, strength and commitment of my inner drive: how determined am I to get through this thing?

- *Viability* is the need to make sure that my goals for where I want to be once I've got through the obstacles in my way are achievable, or else I'm just setting myself up for more trouble when I can't achieve them.

- And *visualisation* is my way of looking forward to those better times and actively working to make them happen rather than just waiting for them to come.

But before we get to those, it's worth looking in closer detail at perhaps the two times in my military career when I most needed resilience: P Company and Selection, the courses to become a Para and an SAS operator respectively. Both of them were unbelievably tough, deliberately so, and no one gets through them without a serious amount of resilience. In fact, that was the single biggest determinant of those who made it and those who didn't. It wasn't who was quickest, fittest or most ripped, and it certainly wasn't who gave it the biggest talk. It was those who were resilient enough to see those courses through to the end as opposed to those who weren't, simple as that.

P Company consisted of eight separate tests over a five-day period:

- a 10-mile march over undulating terrain: I carried a 35 lb bergen and a rifle, and I had to do it in under 1 hr 50 mins;
- the trainasium, an assault course 55 feet above ground which was designed to test my ability to overcome fear and follow simple orders when I was a long way up;
- the log race: eight men carrying a 130 lb log over two miles. This was a bitch, and the DS were watching for determination, aggression and leadership;
- a two-mile march, same kit and weight requirements as the 10-miler, and I had to do this inside 18 minutes;
- the steeplechase, a cross-country run followed by an assault course;
- milling, as I had to do with Beth on *Who Dares Wins*, when I was paired with someone of similar weight and build and given 60 seconds to demonstrate what they term 'controlled physical aggression'. It

was emphatically not boxing, and if I'd used certain boxing moves like blocking or dodging they'd have deducted points. They were looking only for determination and aggression, not skill, technique or even winning or losing. They gave a Golden Handbag award for the recruit who'd shown least of what they were looking for, and though it sounds funny it wasn't the kind of award I wanted anywhere near me if I had any pride or self-respect as a potential Para;

- a 20-mile endurance march, again with the 35 lb bergen and rifle, which had to be done in under four hours and ten minutes;

- and finally the stretcher race, where I had to carry a 175 lb stretcher with three other blokes. It was a five-mile course, but we were swapped in and out on a regular basis.

Take one of those, any one of those, and you'll see that it's pretty tough. Eight of them back to back is really demanding, and made more so by the compound nature of the process. You're not given enough time to recover properly – on purpose, obviously – and so gradually you find yourself getting more and more exhausted. Even if you start P Company full of beans, you'll be hanging out of your arse by the time you're nearing the end; and if you're feeling anything less than good to start with, you're in for a long old five days.

There were plenty of times I needed to dig deep, but three of them really stand out. The first was the two miles in 18 minutes. On paper, this looked one of the easiest exercises, and though I don't think that it lulled me into a false sense of security, I certainly wasn't expecting it to be as rough as it was. Nine minutes a mile isn't too much of an ask on flat tarmac when you're in running kit, though it's a lot quicker than a jog. On undulating hillside wearing assault kit – webbing, day sack, weapon and helmet – it was brutal. There was so little margin for error, and I was out of breath and felt like my lungs were burning from the start. I'm not one of those guys who likes going close to redline when they run – I'd much rather do something ten times as long and go at my own steady pace than be effectively sprinting for close on 20 minutes. Compared with the other exercises this was really short, but in itself 18 minutes is a long time to be absolutely hanging on. And since I was so out of breath I felt that I wasn't really in control of the situation, which in turn made me have to tamp down on any sense of panic that I might not make the cut-off. *Just get through it,* I told myself. *Doesn't matter how bad you look or that you're wheezing away like some grandpa on 60 a day. Just don't come in outside the time limit.* I gritted my teeth, literally as well as metaphorically, and came in with a few seconds to spare.

The second was the milling. Here, my resilience was tested not during the exercise itself but beforehand. Milling is all about psyching yourself up like you would do before battle.

Sixty seconds doesn't sound long, but believe me when you're throwing punches constantly in that time it feels like an hour. Just try it on your own, constantly moving and hitting. If you've got a punchbag then go at that for 60 seconds as hard as you can. You'll feel as though your arms are about to fall off. So I spent hours beforehand psyching myself up into the most aggressive frame of mind I could muster. It was proper raging bull stuff, thinking of all the shit times in my life and how P Company was my chance to escape them and build a new future for myself. I worked myself into such a frenzy that when my turn came I went at my opponent like a wild animal. *Fuck what's coming at you,* I thought, *you just have to keep going towards it. If you get knocked out you get knocked out, but you have to keep going towards it.* He was a boxer, and a decent one too, but like I said they weren't looking for boxers. He kept trying to step inside me, jab and uppercut, all that stuff they teach you in boxing gyms, but I just leathered him

– not because I was bigger, stronger or quicker, but because I was prepared to do what he wasn't.

The final event which really tested me was the 20-miler. This was definitely not just because it was tough in itself (it was, although pro rata from the 10-miler in the same kit it shouldn't have been that much worse, and I'd done that pretty easily), but also because it came so near the end and I had the cumulative effects of everything else already in my body. The resilience I needed here was to settle into a pace I could sustain, know it was going to drag every ounce of energy from me over the next four hours, and accept that this would be the case. I also needed to keep my mindset positive, as being near the end meant I suddenly started thinking of what I had to lose rather than what I had to gain: I'd come so far, I'd done well in the first six events, and to fuck it up this close to the line would have been a bitter pill to swallow.

Curiously, the same thought processes didn't apply in the last event, the stretcher race, even though that was in purely physical terms one of the toughest. Partly this was because I figured that anybody who was going to quit had quit by then, and by this stage we were down to around a quarter of those who'd started basic training five months before. Half had jacked it in even before we made it to P Company, for any number of reasons – they realised this wasn't for them, they were homesick, they wanted to be in a normal unit – and half of those who were left at the start of P Company quit during those five days. I can't remember the exact numbers, but I think we started with around 100, so 50 would have gone before P Company began and another 25 during P Company itself, leaving 25 of us there at the end. This made me feel like part of the elite and gave me so much energy, as though it was a reward for my having hung in there when things had been tough.

Both the stretcher race and the log race also involved teamwork, which I really loved. In the straight endurance and speed courses I was on my own, and when milling I was against someone else, so these were the only two when I had not just to work with others but actively rely on them too. Blokes would drop off both the log and the stretcher, unable to hack the pace, but I was always there, snarling and screaming and absolutely loving it, even though of course the more blokes who dropped off the heavier the load became for the rest. (I was the same in *Who Dares Wins* when we did the log race there. Give me the simplicity of a fuck-off log and I'm happy. I'm aware that this is not normal behaviour.) It wasn't just that I liked being part of a team: I liked being one of the stronger members of that team, driving others on to achieve things they might have thought beyond them.

Hard as it was, P Company was a walk in the park compared to Selection.

There are two main differences between the two. The first and most obvious one is that Selection is much harder and more physically demanding, which shouldn't be much of a surprise. The second is this: most of P Company is done with other people, either in teams (log and stretcher), against them (milling) or at least with lots of other blokes around you (the endurance and speed marches, the trainasium). In Selection, you're much more on your own, which is mentally much harder in itself even before you factor in the greater physical demands.

There are two Selections a year, one in summer and one in winter. You can debate till the cows come home which is harder – people have died on both, from heat exhaustion and hypothermia respectively – but the truth is they're both bloody hard and in the end it really doesn't make much difference, if any.

Selection lasts much longer than P Company: a couple of months as opposed to five days. It doesn't stack the events as closely as P Company does, though there is the final Test Week right at the end, but you're 'on' all the time, and you can be failed or VW (voluntarily withdraw) at any time, not just during the really big events.

We started with a series of timed marches over the Brecon Beacons, including one over the highest peak in the range, Pen y Fan – officially known as the High Walk, but everyone calls it the Fan Dance. Then came the point-to-point marches to test our endurance, map-reading and navigation skills: we went from one point to the next, and at each one we showed the DS the next point we were going to. And finally it was Test Week, where the marches got longer and the loads heavier every day. The two real killers here were trying to navigate through Elan Valley and Endurance, 40 miles with a 70 lb bergen and weapon in 20 hours. If we got through all those ... no, we hadn't passed. All we'd done was book ourselves on the flight to the next phase.

All that lay ahead of me as I drove up to the camp gates with my mate Joe to register ourselves for Selection. I wasn't nervous at all, honestly I wasn't, until we were about ten minutes out, when we suddenly looked at each other and went, 'What the actual fuck are we doing?' That's when it really hit me, the enormity of what I was about to undertake; but almost in the next moment I told myself, 'You're about to put yourself through probably the toughest Special Forces

Selection course in the world. It would be weird if you *weren't* nervous. And remember, nerves are good. Nerves keep you sharp, keep you hungry and keep you from being slack. Nerves help you perform your best.'

Nine of us from 3 Para were doing Selection, so at least I had some familiar faces around me. The DS pulled out all the tricks, all the old classics: having a four-tonner waiting to pick us up, but just as we were about to sling our gear on board and climb up the engine would start up and off the lorry would go. But anyone who wasn't waiting for that to happen was stupid: it was so well known. We were allowed one red flag, as anyone could have a bad day. Mine came early on, when I failed one of the test marches. I'd taken a wrong turn, and though I bust a gut to make it in time I'd gone too far off route and was outside the time limit. The next day we went across three peaks, and I was so revved up, so determined not to fail that I tore a muscle in my foot. It was agony, and each time I put my weight on that foot I felt jagged forks of pain shooting up my leg. My thought process was very simple: *Can I still move? Yes. Then move.* That was all there was to it. I came in 20 minutes under time and near the front of the pack. A lot of blokes missed the time cut on that one, and I thought they'd all be RTU'd (returned to unit: sent back to their own regiments), but because the weather was so bad the DS had pushed the time limit back 10 minutes and some of them stayed. I was spitting mad: not at the blokes themselves, who were just doing what anyone else would have done in that situation and taking any leniency which came their way, but at the DS for moving the goalposts which had resulted in my torn muscles. But when I thought about it more I figured that at least I could say I'd done it properly, and even if that didn't mean anything to anyone else it meant something to me.

God, some of it was hard. It really tested my physical resilience day in, day out, way more than P Company had. Even now, hearing some of the names of the routes we did makes me shudder and smile in equal measure: shudder at how tough they were, smile in satisfaction that I made it through. Gilbert's Gutbuster: 10 miles and at every station we got smashed with hill sprints and press-ups to see who couldn't hack it. That little voice in my head: *Keep going, one foot in front of the other, they can't break you.* The Dicky-Bow Wood: a navigation exercise over the Beacons overseen by a DS who made us take it in turns to lead the group and hammered us so hard that I could hardly remember my own name, let alone a compass bearing, distance and elevation. I thought that one was never going to end. And of course Endurance itself. I was down on time, my leg was agony and I was practically hallucinating with fatigue. *All this way just to fuck it up right at the end? No way. No fucking way.* My whole world had narrowed to this: me, alone on a mountainside, with two and a half hours to make it back in time or be RTU'd. Nothing else mattered. It was success or failure, being someone who'd achieved something or just another knobber who'd been good but not quite good enough. I steeled myself and ran those last two and a half hours. I don't remember much about them other than that my leg stopped hurting and that I had a very clear sensation of pouring everything I had into this, as though all I'd done in my life up to this point was disappearing into a funnel.

Like I said, all this just to get to the next phase. We really must have been gluttons for punishment.

Again, as with P Company, the dropout rate was huge. There were about 180 people at the start, and then a whole load more suddenly appeared in week three who'd been on backfill (a waiting list, basically). And gradually they fell by the wayside. Two things always struck me about the ones who left. First, I could always tell who was going to quit. Always. It was their body language, the way they walked, the way they spoke – not necessarily the words themselves but the tone of voice. There was the tone of the guys who were broken and knew it, there was the tone of the guys who were broken and still trying to deny it, and then there was the tone of the rest of us, and I could tell the difference between the three in half a sentence flat. We'd be pulled out onto a rain-lashed parade ground at four in the morning and the instructor would ask if there was anyone who wanted to quit. I'd wait a second, maybe two, and then I'd hear or see someone walk off. In some ways that was the sensible thing to do: if they weren't going to make it then it was best to save themselves and the DS the bother and just VW. They were doing everyone a favour that way.

And second, I took great energy from those who didn't make it. I mean that literally. We were in big dorms with bunk beds, and every time I'd come back and see another bed empty, sheets and blankets gone and just a bare mattress there, it would feel as though they'd died and I'd got their power. I was a vampire sucking their blood as they died. They were gone, broken, RTU'd, and all the energy they'd had was now mine. If this sounds weird or psycho, rest assured I wasn't the only one who felt that way. The instructors used to call it 'the quickening', after the transfer of power which occurred in the movie *Highlander* whenever one immortal decapitated another. And whatever you called it – vampirism, energy rush, the quickening

– it was always especially acute when the guy who'd fallen by the wayside had been one of the front runners up till then.

I'd never been the strongest or the quickest. I'd needed that willpower more than some of the other guys, the sheer bloody-mindedness to always hang in there no matter what. For once I could turn that struggle to my advantage. There were guys who could hammer a half-marathon or marathon and smoke me, but put them in the harsh environment, make them exist on rations, stick a bergen on their back and make them cover insane distances, and it was a different story. For me that kind of suffering was normal: for them it was extreme.

There are two types of fun, Type One and Type Two. Type One is what we think of when we hear the word 'fun': nights out, bantering with mates, flirting with girls. Type Two is the kind of fun which seems anything but at the time, but which when you're done with it actually gives you a proper sense of achievement and satisfaction. Type One fun can be very forgettable. Type Two never is.

Of the nine from 3 Para who'd started out on Selection, I was the only one who passed. I don't say that by way of conceit or arrogance, but just to illustrate my point. I wasn't the best soldier of that nine, not by a long way. In pretty much any discipline you could think of, there were others better than me. But when it came to resilience I had them all licked, and that's the only reason I stayed in Hereford while they went back to Colchester.

I found out afterwards that I'd done two-thirds of Selection with a bulging disc in my back, and it was that rather than exhaustion which meant that I was practically waddling by the end. It took about three years for it to fully heal, during which time I swam a mile a day to keep the blood flowing to it and dead-lifted tons of weights to build up my core strength. If I'd known during Selection that I'd buggered my back, I wonder if I would have been as resilient as I was in keeping going. Knowing I had a proper medical condition might have given me a mental 'out' and enabled me to make excuses and VW, or maybe not – I believe my wanting to pass far outweighed any injury my body could throw at me. Sometimes, perhaps, it's better not to know these things.

So what did P Company and Selection teach me? How did they help inculcate those seven 'V's I spoke about earlier? It wasn't only those two courses, naturally – there was much more to it than that. Everyone's life is made up of myriad stuff: all the experiences and episodes, all the characteristics and personality traits, which go into making a person who they are. I'm no different. So this is what I've found along the way.

VALUES

Everyone has not just values but core values: those non-negotiable aspects of life which play a huge part in forming their personal identity and which include the things that are most important to them. And everyone's values differ. What you find critical might be of little importance to me: what's a line in the sand for me may be invisible to you. As with the personality types mentioned in 'Self', core values aren't right or wrong (unless they're so obviously wrong as to be immoral or illegal). They just are.

Resilience is fostered by making choices which align with your values. If you make choices which deviate from your values, then your resilience can suffer. Being a Para very much coincided with my core values, which are all the ones I've used as a structure for this book: leadership, excellence and so on. Field Marshal Montgomery, one of Britain's most famous military leaders, once asked rhetorically:

What manner of men are these who wear the maroon red beret? They are firstly all volunteers, and are then toughened by hard physical training. As a result they have that infectious optimism and that offensive eagerness which comes from physical well-being. They have jumped from the air and by doing so have conquered fear. Their duty lies in the van of the battle: they are proud of this honour and have never failed in any task. They have the highest standards in all things, whether it be skill in battle or smartness in the execution of all peace time duties. They have shown themselves to be as tenacious and determined in defence as they are courageous in attack. They are, in fact, men apart – every man an Emperor.

Toughened, optimistic, proud, tenacious, determined, courageous – I couldn't have written it better myself. If being a Para was good enough for Monty, it was good enough for me. Or at least that's what I thought until I joined The Regiment. Oh, don't get me wrong: I was hugely proud to be a Para and always will be. But though my own core values coincided with those of the Paras, they didn't end there. When I first joined the Paras I'd see the guys who'd gone on Selection – not the ones who'd passed, just the ones who'd tried – and I'd think of them as legends. It didn't matter that they'd failed and been RTU'd – even to go and try out was an achievement, as the CO had to release them and he wouldn't release someone he thought had no chance. But when I passed Selection, I thought of them as a bit weak, because by then I'd moved on and past them. One of my core values is striving: I'm never satisfied with what I've done, and I always want more. Knowing this allows me to be resilient while pursuing it. It also allows me to be at peace with myself when I move on. 3 Para was a massive part of my life, but apart from one time to pick up my stuff I've never been back to Colchester barracks since I left the unit. As the Greek philosopher Heraclitus said, you can never step in the same river twice, as the river isn't the same and neither are you.

VALIDATION

If you find that you're struggling to get through something tough, it helps to think of times in the past when you've been faced with a similar situation and managed to come through it. Within reason, it's true that what doesn't kill you makes you stronger. Whatever it was that you faced, remember what it was and how you coped with it. You may have coped with it imperfectly, or hesitantly, or even only partially. That doesn't matter.

The fact is that you did cope with it, and you're still here and still fighting. That's what matters.

Some people tend to dismiss or downplay past struggles by telling themselves that whatever it was, it could have been worse. 'Well, at least I wasn't starving in Africa.' 'He only ever shouted at me, never hit me.' That kind of thing, often dressed up in sardonic throwaway lines like, 'Worse things happen at sea.' All these things may be true: they're also irrelevant. If something was a stressor then the stress it caused you was valid. If everybody compared themselves with everybody else then nobody would ever acknowledge any of their own suffering, as there's always someone worse off than you are.

If you suffered then you were tested, it's as simple as that. Just as those fast runners didn't know how to properly suffer until the continuation training broke them, so too people who've never been really tested are more likely to come unstuck when they finally do face a serious challenge. But if you have experience of such a challenge then you can use the lessons you learned last time to face this one with more confidence and skill. Since by definition you didn't break last time, why should you break this time? You were strong then and you are strong now.

You can also find validation through more general affirmations of your strengths, not necessarily those purely connected to hard times in the past. Think of any and every success you've had. It doesn't matter how small it was or in what area of your life it came, just that it meant something to you at the time: scoring the winning goal in a school hockey match, getting a job you'd gone for, completing a charity walk, anything like that. Successes are proof that you have talent and drive. If need be, write down a list of these achievements, along with anything important that they taught you. In the early days of his career, the Welsh and Lions rugby captain Sam Warburton used to keep a PDF on his phone called 'Warby's Winning Ways'. It was a short document with pictures of him in the heat of battle, positive newspaper reviews, glowing testimonials from his team-mates, coaches and former teachers, and even the logos of his sponsors as a reminder that these companies felt that he was worth investing in. He would refer to it whenever he needed some positive affirmation, whenever he found himself doubting his ability or ground down by the relentless pressure of being a professional sportsman; and though after a while he found he didn't need it anymore, he still adhered to the principle behind its creation in the first place. *There's a reason why you're picked, there's a reason why you do this for a living.*

I did something similar many times, though in my head rather than on paper. Standing by the open door of an aircraft about to do a night jump, as I mentioned in 'Danger', what did I think? *You're in the fucking SAS.* Those five words weren't just a statement of the bleeding obvious – there was a whole lot of life credo behind them. *You're in the fucking SAS. As in: You've spent years honing your craft. You've come all the way from that skinny kid walking into the army recruiting office to being a Tier One operator. Of all the tens of millions of soldiers around the world, you're among the top fraction of 1 per cent. You've trained not just hard and smart. You surround yourself with excellence every day. You wouldn't have got anywhere near this level, let alone stayed there year on year, unless people thought you were worthy of it.*

Now get out the door and fucking jump.

VIEWPOINT

It's very easy when faced with a challenging situation to see it only from the most immediate point of view; that is, right in front of you. When something's right in front of you it looms large, sometimes larger than it actually is. When Liverpool beat AC Milan on penalties in the 2005 Champions League final, the Liverpool keeper Jerzy Dudek made sure to stand near the penalty spot on his way to the goal. Sometimes he'd even hand the ball to the Milan player about to take the penalty. It was a clever thing to do: Dudek was making himself look huge and the goal behind him look small simply by placing himself right in the opponent's face and letting perspective do the rest. But in actual fact Dudek was 6 ft 2 in and the goal was 24 ft × 8 ft. One was much, much bigger than the other. It was Dudek's smart thinking which neutralised or even reversed that perception in the minds of the Milan players.

Changing your viewpoint can greatly help with resilience. Even if you're facing a situation which seems so serious as to be both all-consuming and permanent, occupying almost all your thoughts all of the time, you can still put it into perspective by stepping away from the immediate viewpoint and looking at it from another angle. I've found that three things have worked for me: stepping forward, stepping aside and stepping back.

Stepping forward involves imagining looking back at this moment from some time in the future. I pick a spot a few months or years down the line, when not just the situation itself but the effects will have faded. How will I feel about the situation then? I know I'll feel differently, because the intense emotions which currently accompany that situation will have faded and I'll be able to look back on it rationally and even with amusement at certain aspects. It doesn't matter what the situation actually is. It can be professional or personal: perhaps a difficult time at work or the break-up of a long-term relationship. What matters is that at a certain point in the future this situation will have been resolved and the intensity of negative emotions and distress will have faded. Imagining my future self looking back at today is really helpful, because I know that on some level I'll be thinking, 'Well, that wasn't so bad, was it? And certainly not worth getting so worked up about.'

I might even have changed my life so drastically that this will seem almost to have happened in another existence, or found that what I thought was so bad at the time had unexpected silver linings. If you find this hard to imagine, then remember that you already have evidence that this works from the previous point, 'validation': you're now in a place where you can look back with equanimity on past traumas, so it follows that one day you'll be able to treat this current one the same way. Almost anything can be recast in a different light if you're imaginative enough to consider that and resourceful enough to go through with making the necessary changes. When soldiers are severely wounded in conflict, for example, their injuries are routinely referred to as 'life-changing', with the implication that the change is negative. And indeed that change will be negative if they let it be. But imagine lying in hospital with a leg missing and imagining how those changes might be viewed as positive in five years' time: a career as a wheelchair athlete, a new outlet in motivational speaking, a greater appreciation of things you once took for granted. This is not sugar-coating or soft-soaping some serious and real trauma, simply applying a different viewpoint to it. People talk about knock-backs, but why not knocksideways? Not a regression, but a new direction.

Stepping aside involves exactly what it says: looking at this moment from the side. Imagine standing on a railway line and watching a train coming towards you. All you can see is the front of that train – you have no idea how long or short it is, just that it's in your face and a problem you have to deal with. Now imagine stepping off that track, walking 100 metres or so to the side, and looking at the train again. You'll not only see the train moving, but you'll also see the last carriage where it ends. The train might be a three-carriage subur-ban passenger train or a mile-long freight train, it doesn't matter. What matters is that it has an end and that you can see it. The train, like the situation, doesn't last for ever.

This is different from stepping forward in an impor-tant way. Stepping forward involves casting a long way into the future when not just the situation but its effects have been resolved. Stepping aside is a much more immediate reminder that the situation is temporary, and sometimes this short-term thinking is what you need. Stepping aside doesn't require you to think about the long-term effects, just the present and immediate future. Stepping aside is at heart about four words: *this, too, will pass*.

Ultramarathoners do this all the time. They like to talk about the pain cave, when the pain is all they can think about. The pain cave is an extraordinary place: strange, special and pure. If you run an ultra you both find yourself and lose yourself in the pain cave, because that's what you came here for. Its contours are jagged and sharp, and just as Friedrich Nietzsche wrote, 'When you look into the abyss, the abyss looks back into you,' so too the pain cave looks straight back into you, narrowing and shrink-wrapping itself around you. There's no way around it, only through it; and when you reach the exit it's like finding a rose growing out of concrete. But that's the crucial part: you *do* reach the exit. The pain cave has an entrance and an exit, and it doesn't last for ever.

Finally, *stepping back*. Stepping back is accepting that some things just happen and can't be controlled. We're so used in life to being able to control things, and we so want to control as much as possible, that it's hard to accept that sometimes we just can't. You can control the controllables, but the rest is out of your hands, and you'll find that accepting this makes you more resilient rather than less so. Whatever you resist persists. Look at all the people on *Who Dares Wins* who burned up energy trying to work out who the mole was. None of them were still there at the end. The stronger contestants were the ones who realised that worrying about the mole was counterproductive for three reasons. First, there was nothing they could do about it. Second, they should be behaving at all times in a way that would encourage the mole to give them positive reports to the DS. Finally, the course required every ounce of resilience those people had, and wasting even an ounce of that resilience on something out of their control was at best stupid and at worst the difference between passing and failing.

You're waiting for a flight and it's delayed. What to do? Ranting and raving is going to make no difference to whether or not the flight takes off, but lots of difference to your mood, energy reserves and resilience if you're forced to sleep on the airport floor for a night. You're stuck in traffic and are going to be late for a meeting. Same thing. Yelling abuse at other drivers won't make the traffic move any quicker, and will just ensure that when you do get to that meeting you're flustered and agitated. Stepping back gives you the resilience not just to deal with these setbacks but also repurpose them. Use the time to do something useful such as reading a book or listening to a podcast.

All three tactics – stepping forward, stepping aside and stepping back – have the same effect. They help stop you from seeing yourself as a victim, someone to whom bad things inevitably happen and who can't help but suffer as a result. The truly resilient person never sees themselves as a victim. Victimhood is a mindset. The more you see yourself as a victim the more you'll become one, because that mindset is self-reinforcing: you're in a bad situation, you take no steps either to cope with it or get out of it, so the situation persists or worsens, making it even harder for you to cope, and so on. It's easy to get stuck thinking about negative outcomes, asking ourselves what we could have done differently in the past and wondering how we'll find ways to screw up in the future. Ruminating like this won't help us solve our problems: it just means that our thoughts go round and round like a hamster on a wheel and sends us careering towards catastrophisation, when we start not just to consider the worst possible outcome to a situation but actively expect it, and in a weird way even welcome it as it would prove that we were right all along. This is not sensible worst-case-scenario planning

– it's something much more insidious and corrosive. And there's no point trying to solve problems with the same thinking that created them; resilient people don't make the same mistake again and again, because they're willing to be honest about why they failed and to think about what didn't work. So just as being a victim is a mindset, so too is not being a victim also a mindset, and that mindset is resilience.

VARIANTS

There are no hard and fast rules for how to be resilient: no one size fits all, no magic formula. What works for one person might not work for another, what works for you in one situation may not work for you in another, and what worked before may not work now and vice versa. The concept of resilience is a complex one, and resilience exists on a continuum that presents itself in differing degrees across multiple domains of life. For example, you may be very resilient in the workplace but much less so in your personal life, perhaps because you find it hard to deal with strong emotions which are triggered much more easily at home than at work.

So you need to find what works for you, which often involves playing to your strengths. Yes, it's always good to work on your weaknesses, but when times are tough the last thing you need is to be trying to deal with that kind of improvement on top of everything else. So play to your strengths and use them to help get you through. Again, everyone's strengths differ, but one of the things I've found most useful is exercise.

Exercise is self-medication in a good way. There's self-medication in a bad way, which is too much alcohol or drugs; these only mask the feelings of stress rather than dealing with the causes of them head-on. Exercise for me has two main benefits when it comes to dealing with stressful situations and promoting resilience: general and specific.

The general benefits of exercise are manifold. Being physically fit enables me to approach tough times with confidence, as stress is one of the biggest causes of ailments. The fitter I am, the more able to deal with stress I feel. Stress can increase blood pressure and heart rates, so the lower these are to start with the better. Fitness gives me more energy, which again can get zapped in times which require resilience. And keeping fit also encourages me to look after myself in other ways: eating properly, sleeping properly, staying hydrated, not drinking too much booze. Physical health is the base on which I build all the other pillars of my life: it's my underpinning, my foundation.

The specific benefits of exercise are more an

immediate reaction to a given situation. If I'm feeling stressed, confused or on the cusp of being overwhelmed, exercise is my reset button. I go for a long bike ride or run, or a sea swim, or do a workout with weights, or have sparring sessions with a mate. When I'm working hard physically, it clears my head – I feel the stress draining away with the sweat. And by putting my brain in neutral at times like these, I often find that the answer to a problem presents itself far quicker and more easily than if I'd just sat there and stewed about it. Exercise doesn't even have to be hard and on the redline. A few miles' walk across a heath or along clifftops is just as cleansing: being outside and among nature is hugely important to me, feeling the sun and wind on my face, and staying away from screens which just clutter my mind with distractions and useless info. That kind of mental break through active solitude is critical in helping me through things.

Exercise apart, I find two other things that help. I try not to be afraid of my emotions. It's easy to shy from negative emotions as they're uncomfortable and can feel draining, particularly at times when you're already going through the mill, but actually it's more important to let them come through you and deal with them. When I got to the top of Everest the second time, I cried. I hadn't cried the first time, as that had been so easy I hadn't felt particularly challenged, but the second time was so different. I'd had to dig very deep within myself after all the difficulties along the way, and shedding a tear on top of the world was both a reaction to and part of the resilience that I'd needed to access.

Finally, I always find that a sense of humour really helps. This is perhaps also part of the previous section, 'Viewpoint', but it's also a good thing to have in life generally. Sometimes things get so bad that all you can do is laugh. Laughter doesn't just create positivity and bond you with other people, both of which are part of resilience; it also reminds you not to take things so seriously. Army humour in particular is very dark, but that doesn't mean that soldiers are uncaring or callous – that's just our way of dealing with things, and when you've seen some dark stuff, which we all have, you need an equally black sense of humour to deal with it. Police, medical personnel and firefighters are the same. If you have the resilience to get through tough situations together, you can talk to those who were there with you in ways which can shock those who weren't. There's a story about a Marine who stepped on a landmine in the Falklands and had his leg blown off. One of his mates started to tourniquet the wound and tried to comfort the injured man, who was very distressed. 'I've lost my leg,' he kept saying. 'I've lost my fucking leg.'

'No, you haven't,' came the reply. 'It's over there.'

Trust me, the memory of that line would have made the wounded soldier laugh – not at the time, sure, but when in rehab facing a seismic change to his life, most definitely. And in laughing he'd have known that his mate cared, and that would have helped give him the strength to persevere.

VEHEMENCE

How much do you want something? How deep and hard are you prepared to go to achieve it? The vehemence of your inner drive is crucial in determining whether or not you have the resilience to see things through. As the old saying goes, winners never quit and quitters never win. Failure is not falling down, but refusing to get up.

I showed this on both P Company and Selection. Right from the start I decided that I would do anything to get through, and this involved channelling everything into keeping my inner focus pure and bright. All I concerned myself with was my own performance, not those of other people. I realised that looking around me was a hiding to nothing and would just risk denting my resilience. Watching someone weaker might just tempt me to follow their lead and jack it in; watching someone stronger might dispirit me and make me think I would never be as good as that, so why even bother trying?

So through good times and bad, I just kept my eyes on the prize. It was actually very simple: this is what you need to do, this is what it will take to achieve it, so just concentrate on that. All the hurt and pain and suffering: suck it up, buttercup. I knew that even when I thought I was at my absolute limit I would still have more to give. Scientists believe that our perceived limits are somewhere between 40 and 60 per cent of our actual limits, and that therefore we're actually nowhere near the ultimate frontier of what we can achieve; that in effect the brain puts up barriers to stop the body from further pain. It's like a motorbike having a main petrol tank and a reserve one too, so that when one is empty you can switch to the other. You always have more.

That said, there were plenty of people who wanted it too much, or if not exactly too much then definitely in the wrong way, in an unhealthy way. There were blokes, especially on Selection, who'd turned their whole lives over to it, who'd given up their marriages and the like just to have a shot at it. They were obsessed with it, absolutely obsessed, and it was really annoying for everyone else. I know I spoke about not letting yourself get into the Plan B mindset, but that only really works effectively if the rest of your life is on a vaguely even keel and you have a solid platform to work off. If you've put all your eggs in a single basket, not just professionally but personally too, that's a recipe for disaster. As John Candy's coach character says about an Olympic gold medal in the movie *Cool Runnings*: 'If you're not enough without it, you'll never be enough with it.'

VIABILITY

There's no quicker way to dent your resilience than to set yourself impossible goals. You'll never achieve them, and in trying to do so you'll set yourself up for inevitable disappointment. That rather American mantra, 'You can do anything you want to do, you can be anything you want to be,' just isn't true. It's true that you can do a lot more than you think, and that you can excel in the right field for you, but if nothing else you have to take genetics into account. I could have set my heart on being the best tennis player in the world, but no matter how hard or smart I'd trained I'd never have made it. I just don't have the hand–eye co-ordination needed at that level, and nothing could change that (apart from having had different parents).

So if you want to maximise resilience on the way towards achieving your goal, that goal has to be a SMART one: specific, measurable, achievable, relevant and time-bound.

- *Specific.* It's no use wanting to be 'the best you can be'. That's amorphous, ambiguous and too easy to fudge. Instead, make your goal something narrow and specific: such as becoming a member of the SAS.

- *Measurable.* If you can't measure a goal, how do you know whether you've achieved it or not? I could have reasonably aimed at being the best soldier in the British army, or one of the top 100 soldiers in the world, but how would I ever have known? There are no rankings, no awards, no trophies.

- *Achievable.* As with the tennis example above, a goal has to be achievable, or else it will remain a pipe dream and therefore marooned in the realms of fantasy rather than reality. It can be a difficult goal – most goals worth reaching are – but you have to have a chance of making it.

- *Relevant.* A goal has to be relevant to your life, which means it has to be in accordance both with your core values and your interests. Trying to achieve something which does not energise, interest or validate you is a waste of time and effort. I wanted to climb Everest because it was relevant to me in every way.

- *Time-bound*. We don't have an infinite amount of time on this earth, and so you have to set limits on your goals. Improvement may be a never-ending process, but specific goals aren't. At some stage you have to think, 'Well, if I haven't got to this stage by this point in time then maybe I'm barking up the wrong tree.' One of the reasons I like mountaineering is that time is of the essence when summiting high peaks: once the weather window's over it's over and there's nothing you can do about it, so you concentrate all your efforts in that window and accept when it's done.

VISUALISATION

Visualising positive outcomes to tough situations is helpful in several ways.

First, it helps you work out what exactly you want to achieve out of the situation – what, precisely, will constitute your definition of success. If you're struggling through a painful break-up with a partner, visualise what you'll regard as a positive outcome. Will it be when the two of you can be friends again? When your feelings have faded enough for you not to have an involuntary reaction on hearing their name or seeing their picture? When the decree absolute comes through and you never have to see them again? It doesn't matter what that positive is, only that you can visualise it – walking out of court for the last time, sitting in a pub with them and being uncomplicatedly happy to see them without any other considerations – and so know what you have to work towards.

Second, the act of visualisation itself gives you increased positivity, as the brain responds well to the actual imagining and sends positive chemicals to the body. Your psychological exercise has physiological effects. It's like the old saying, 'Fake it till you make it.' If you see yourself in those positive scenarios, then you will start feeling the same kind of emotions that you would feel if you were in those scenarios for real.

Third, envisaging specific aspects of the situation which have yet to happen makes you better equipped to deal with them when they do happen. When I climbed Everest, I thought in advance about certain parts of the climb that I knew would be difficult, such as the Khumbu Icefall and the Hillary Step. I envisaged myself not just climbing them but overcoming them too, so that when it actually came to do those parts I felt that I was in control of the situation and not reacting to something new, scary, unexpected and difficult at a time when I most needed to be smart and resilient.

EPILOGUE

People often ask what advice I'd go back and give my younger self. I never really know how to answer that question, as I'm not sure my younger self would have listened to anything I'd told him. The one thing I am sure of is that, if you'd said he'd end up writing a book about his military career and applying the lessons learned there to life in general, he'd have thought you were taking the piss, properly mental, or both. But here I am, and that alone should show you what's possible if you work hard enough and, just as importantly, if you work smart enough.

I don't know exactly what my future holds beyond a few basic pillars. I know that next year I'll be racing Praga cars: the races are an hour long and we'll work in teams of two. I know that I'll be running at least one company, but maybe more. I know that I'll still be setting myself crazy challenges just to see if I can do them and to get the buzz from completing them. I had hoped to do something like that in the autumn of 2020, but for one reason and another it didn't happen. It's a bespoke and rather extreme triathlon, but I'll keep the details under wraps for now as it's something I'd still love to do.

Here's what I *do* know, though:

- I know that I'll still be doing things which align with my self-image and core values.
- I know that I'll still be open to opportunities whenever and wherever they arise.
- I know that I'll still be providing as much leadership as I can to whoever needs it.
- I know that I'll still be putting myself in danger, because that's when I feel most alive.
- I know that I'll still be using my intelligence in all its forms to keep improving my life.
- I know that I'll still be seeking excellence in every aspect of that life.
- And I know that I'll still be practising resilience, because I'll always need it.

In other words, I know that, in all the ways which really matter, I'll still be a soldier.